WHAT PEOPLE

WITCHCR

Sixty years after the publication of *Witchcraft Today*, we have seen Gerald Gardner's vision grow and evolve as it spreads around the globe. *Witchcraft Today – 60 Years On* is a fitting tribute, bringing together authors from different paths within the Craft, each with a unique contribution and insight to inspire those who are practising, teaching, and strengthening Wicca today and for the generations to come.

Dr Vivianne Crowley, Faculty of Pastoral Counseling and Chaplaincy, Cherry Hill Seminary

Witchcraft Today – 60 Years On is a comprehensive look at the evolution of modern witchcraft. It takes you on a magical journey through the popular traditions practiced today, as well as veering off into the mystical realms of cottage witchery and kitchen witchery, exploring the natural world of the wise-woman. This book doesn't only draw from a rich history of what was to become modern pagan practices, but it looks into the future of one of the fastest growing spirituality movements of our time.

Amythyst Raine-Hatayama, author, *The Gray Witch's Grimoire*

An engrossing and eye opening collection of pieces that would startle Gardner himself in their diversity. As a witch myself, raised by parents who both experienced Paganism through Wicca, ceremonial magic and natural witchcraft, Paganism is a natural part of my life. Reading these stories of how others have reached the same point in their lives is both reassuring and inspirational. This book has made me think about my own roots, the experiences of my mentor, and the impact Gardner has had on the continuing evolution of witchcraft; today, tomorrow, and into the future.

Mabh Savage, Celtic Witch and author of *A Modern Celt*

Witchcraft Today
~ 60 Years On

Witchcraft Today
~ 60 Years On

Edited by

Trevor Greenfield

Winchester, UK
Washington, USA

First published by Moon Books, 2014
Moon Books is an imprint of John Hunt Publishing Ltd., Laurel House, Station Approach,
Alresford, Hants, SO24 9JH, UK
office1@jhpbooks.net
www.johnhuntpublishing.com
www.moon-books.net

For distributor details and how to order please visit the 'Ordering' section on our website.

Text copyright: Trevor Greenfield 2013

ISBN: 978 1 78279 168 3

A CIP catalogue record for this book is available from the British Library.

Design: Stuart Davies
www.stuartdaviesart.com

Printed and bound by CPI Group (UK) Ltd, Croydon, CR0 4YY

We operate a distinctive and ethical publishing philosophy in all
areas of our business, from our global network of authors to
production and worldwide distribution.

CONTENTS

Preface

One of the pleasures of being the Publisher of Moon Books is coming into contact with so many interesting people whose beliefs and interests span not only the entire range of the Pagan spectrum, but which also reflect the diversity that exists within each individual tradition. Nowhere is this more obvious than in Witchcraft / Wicca where, in the sixty years following Gardner's publication of *Witchcraft Today*, new paths have appeared, and older ones emerged out of the shadow of repression and illegality, to express with a new and more confident voice their beliefs and practice, sharing, with a steadily growing audience, their knowledge, their certainties, their questions and their vision. This book is a celebration of some of the many paths that Witchcraft / Wicca has taken and of the journeys that people have embarked upon. We hope you enjoy it.

Trevor Greenfield

Introduction

Witchcraft Today, by Gerald Gardner, was published in 1954 making it sixty years to date and bearing in mind that the witch-craft laws had not long been repealed it was quite an achievement. Reading his original book gives us a glorious peek through the looking glass to see how the Craft was back then.

My particular favourite part of his original book is the opening paragraph which states:

> I have been told by witches in England: 'Write and tell people we are not perverts. We are decent people, we only want to be left alone, but there are certain secrets that you mustn't give away.' So after some argument as to exactly what I must not reveal, I am permitted to tell much that has never before been made public concerning their beliefs, their rituals and their reasons for what they do; also to emphasise that neither their present beliefs, rituals nor practices are harmful.

Unfortunately, we still see those beliefs in some people today that don't understand or have any idea about witches. Sadly, persecution of those following the Craft still happens. However the 'secret' side of the Craft has been blown wide open not only with the amount of books now available but with the invention of the internet, I don't believe there are any secrets left! I wonder if Gardner ever expected the Craft to be so open and wide spread.

When I first came to the Craft most of the information available was on Wicca and a huge amount of that stemmed from Gardner and whether you like and respect his work or not you have to admit he was a pioneer for modern witchcraft, he brought it to the attention of the masses and made it accessible to the public, sixty years on and his books are still selling and can be found on the shelf of your local library. In fact Gardner makes the solid point in his book that Witchcraft is available to all people, quite a bold statement then but a very true one. By that he meant that we all have the power and inner energy to work with magic and witchcraft but I think the statement also mirrors how the art and knowledge of witchcraft is now so freely available to everyone.

Obviously, he wasn't the very first witch but he took the knowledge and experience he gained from working with witches and formalised it, bringing the information together and, of course, adding a large amount of his own thoughts and ideas to it and giving it a structure. He set the wheels in motion for what has turned out to be a huge revolution.

My original training was in Wicca, I have worked through the three Wiccan degrees and even my title of High Priestess originates, even if only in part, from Gardner. Although now my pathway has twisted and turned and branched away from Wicca and along the less formal and ceremonial lines of Kitchen and Hedge Witchcraft my Wiccan training gave me a good grounding in the basics and structure of the Craft.

Now we have a vast array of different pagan pathways and a lot of them are covered in this new *Witchcraft Today* book, but within most of them you will see at least some remnants of Gardner's teachings right through to almost word for word followings of them.

This new book not only gives a perspective on witchcraft as we know it today but also how each pathway evolved and where it came from. Each author that has written for this book shares their own personal experiences from their individual journeys with the Craft and it is easy to see how Gardner affected the pathways that they are on, it is a fascinating read.

From Gardner you have, of course, Gardnerian Witchcraft but from that you have Alexandrian then this book also takes you on a journey through Seax, Eclectic Wicca, Dianic, Hekatean,

Egyptian and all the various traditional Old Ways such as Hedge Witchcraft and Solitary Witchcraft, Witchcraft from a male point of view and even how Witchcraft may possibly evolve in the future, so many different views in one book but all interestingly with common themes running through them.

This book is a celebration of Witchcraft, a hat tip to Gerald Gardner and a testimony to the wonderful pathways within the Craft that we walk and how wonderfully diversified, individual and personal they all are but also how many similarities they have. Gerald Gardner was definitely a visionary. I wonder how the Craft will have changed in sixty years from now. This book is a marker for that, looking at the changes over the last sixty years so that we have a reference point to work back to, almost like a Witchcraft timeline to follow.

Whether you are new to the Craft or whether you have walked the pagan pathway for many years the work and promotion that Gerald Gardner did for witchcraft has to be acknowledged and you will see glimpses of it within many aspects of modern Witchcraft. As we move forward it would be lovely to take the ground breaking work he did and continue to share and illuminate the truth of this wonderful faith, religion and lifestyle that we have across the world.

Rachel Patterson

Part I

Forms, Themes & Values

The Making of 'Witchcraft Today'

Philip Heselton

When Gerald Gardner was initiated in September 1939 into what he called "the witch cult", his immediate response was to announce: "People must be told about it! We mustn't let it die!" But, as Gardner found out:

> ...witches are shy people, and publicity is the last thing they want. I asked the first one I knew: "Why do you keep all this wonderful knowledge secret? There is no persecution nowadays. " I was told: "Isn't there? If it were known in the village what I am, every time anyone's chickens died, every time a child became sick, I should be blamed. Witchcraft doesn't pay for broken windows!" [Gerald B Gardner – *Witchcraft Today* – Rider 1954 p18]

But Gerald didn't give up. As his initiate, Patricia Crowther, says:

> ...having been a close friend of Gerald's, I knew he could be very persuasive and convincing in his ideas. ... he had not wanted to see the Craft die out. And how were people to become interested in it, if they did not know it still existed? [Patricia Crowther – Foreword to *High Magic's Aid* – Pentacle Enterprises edition 1993 p1]

The idea of fiction as a medium to put over certain principles of the Craft (as the "witch cult" was also known) probably came to Gerald after the initial refusal. He had some experience of writing fiction in his novel *A Goddess Arrives* [Stockwell 1939]. Eventually Gerald got the permission he needed:

... as it is a dying cult, I thought it was a pity that all the knowledge should be lost, so in the end I was permitted to write, as fiction, something of what a witch believes, in the novel, *High Magic's Aid*. [*Witchcraft Today* pp18-19]

He had a freer hand in a work of fiction to give details of witch beliefs and practices without it being obvious that they were other than pure invention. Unless the hint was given that it was something more, the book could be read as a simple historical adventure story with elements of magic and witchcraft woven into it. At the same time, it could perform the function of an introductory guide to the "Craft of the Wise" – the only one available – and Gerald could give copies to those whom he thought ready to receive it.

Whilst Gerald achieved a lot of what he wanted to with *High Magic's Aid*, he was obviously limited because it was a work of fiction, and he couldn't therefore make the statement that he wanted to make – that witches still existed and moreover that he was an initiated witch himself – though those visiting the museum that he helped to run on the Isle of Man would get a very clear idea about that. Some of the exhibits were specifically captioned as coming from present-day witch covens, and the notice that was on display at the table where Gerald was selling *High Magic's Aid* made it quite clear that witches still existed.

The turning point was in January 1952, when a book by Pennethorne Hughes was published with the simple title of *Witchcraft*. In many ways it was just a typical history largely based on the works of Margaret Murray, but the consequences of its publication were very far-reaching indeed.

When they read the book, the witches who initiated Gerald were considerably disturbed by it, the following being a typical passage:

... witchcraft, as a cult-belief in Europe, is dead. As a

degenerate form of a primitive fertility belief, incorporating the earliest instructive wisdom, the practice is over. Conjurers, wisewomen, palmists, and perverts may be called witches, but it is using an old stick to beat a dead dog. [Pennethorne Hughes – *Witchcraft* – Longmans Green 1952 p204]

One can well imagine their reaction to being equated with degeneracy, perverts and dead dogs, and how this would not exactly enamour them with Hughes!

If they had been somewhat ambivalent about giving Gerald permission to write his book, they were made more determined that he should go ahead by an article that appeared in the weekly magazine, *Illustrated*, in the issue dated 27th September 1952 under the title of "Witchcraft in Britain", which was actually mostly about the practice of black magic. It was just the sort of thing that made them angry, with its misrepresentation of witchcraft. It made them more determined than ever to encourage Gerald in his endeavours, though it is clear that they wanted to be very much in the background.

The witches were angry, indeed incensed, by the way this article and Hughes' book gave a totally distorted view of the witches' beliefs and practices, but what could they do? They were in something of a quandary. On the one hand, the Cult was secret and they didn't want people even to know of its existence. Yet, here was an author who was giving what appeared to be a most warped view of the Cult, which made them angry.

Since the publication of *High Magic's Aid*, Gerald had been pestering them to write something of a more factual nature about the Cult. It would need careful thinking and a lot of talking about what could and could not be mentioned, but they agreed to his writing the factual book on the Cult that he had long wanted to produce.

This [Hughes' *Witchcraft*] made some of my friends very

angry, and I managed to persuade them that it might do good to write a factual book about witchcraft, and so I wrote *Witchcraft Today*. [G B Gardner – *The Meaning of Witchcraft* – Aquarian 1959 p12]

We don't know exactly when those discussions took place, certainly at the latest by June 1952. In the Foreword to *Witchcraft Today*, Gerald gives some detail:

I have been told by witches in England: "Write and tell people we are not perverts. We are decent people, we only want to be left alone, but there are certain secrets that you mustn't give away". So, after some argument as to exactly what I must not reveal, I am permitted to tell much that has never before been made public concerning their beliefs, their rituals and their reasons for what they do ... [*Witchcraft Today* – p13]

They were quite adamant about what they would and wouldn't allow. They particularly did not want Gerald to give details of any rituals that were definitely magical, nor did they wish it to be known how they raised power. Gerald described the situation:

... I soon found myself between Scylla and Charybdis. If I said too much, I ran the risk of offending people whom I had come to regard highly as friends. If I said too little, the publishers would not be interested. In this situation I did the best I could. [*The Meaning of Witchcraft* – p12]

Gerald got down to writing quickly after receiving the initial permission, in case they changed their minds. This is reflected in an early version of his Foreword, where he writes:

... I want to get it out before I am told: "It doesn't matter; let it go, don't write anything." [Gerald Gardner – *New Light on*

Witchcraft – (manuscript in Toronto collection)]

Gerald had certainly started writing the book by August 1952. In fact, he had probably been working on such a book for several years. Indeed, in a sense, his whole life and his interest in and wide reading around a large number of topics had been preparation for what in many ways would become his "magnum opus".

Anyway, within these guidelines, we can imagine that Gerald started work on the manuscript of a book which was initially to be entitled "New Light on Witchcraft".

He was now free, within certain limits, to write what he wanted to, but, after the initial euphoria, he found fairly quickly that merely giving the witches' beliefs and non-magical practices resulted in a very short manuscript. The problem was that what they told him tended to slip through his fingers. Much was non-verbal and he probably forgot a lot. By late 1952 and early 1953, when the bulk of the book was being written, he was living on the Isle of Man, away from regular contact with Dafo (Edith Woodford-Grimes), whom I suspect to be the only one of the original group with whom he was still in touch.

Witchcraft Today is not just an account of Gerald's contact with the witches and of their beliefs and practices. It isn't even *mainly* about that: in fact, probably less than 10% of the book is about the thoughts and activities of the witches that Gerald claimed to have met. I think the problem was that, when he came to write about what the witches told him, he found it difficult because it had been in no sense a structured course of learning – more things told at odd times in a strange order and he wasn't very good at remembering. Anyway, he set things down as best he could.

Nevertheless, there wasn't enough material to make a book on its own, so Gerald gave himself a free hand to write about his own ideas and theories about the development of witchcraft, including much historical material. The information about the witches he had met was scattered about the book like plums in a pudding. In fact, just as plums might tend to sink to the bottom, so much of this material seems to be included in Chapter 13 – Recapitulation – which is almost an afterthought, as if he suddenly realised that there was material on the witches that he had forgotten about and hadn't included and that therefore he had to cram it in the final chapter, probably at the last minute.

Anyway, it became clear that he needed to supplement the text with other material. And Gerald was far from short of material. Here was a blank canvas on which he could speculate.

The bulk of the book is really a summation of Gerald's reading on witchcraft and allied subjects over a number of years. What I think he was aiming to do was to provide an outline history of witchcraft, from the Stone Age onwards, at the same time showing the connections that certain religious or other groups may have had with the Craft. This gave him the opportunity to write about many of his favourite topics, including the Druids, the "Little People", the Knights Templar, Ancient Egypt, the Greek Mysteries and much more besides. In many ways, *Witchcraft Today* is a record of Gerald's phases of enthusiasm.

Gerald was an exponent of the idea that the fairies, or Little People, that were the subject of legend and folklore, particularly in the Celtic countries, were actually the older and original inhabitants of those lands who were marginalised by later invaders. He presented as evidence the small size of many remains of dwellings and that the Little People were supposed to live in conical hills, in effect round-houses. He sums them up by saying:

> All these people seem to be remembered by the same characteristics: good friends but dangerous enemies, very strong, able to disappear at will, having great festivals at night and making use of poisoned arrows. [*Witchcraft Today* – p59]

Whatever the truth of this idea, it has other exponents, but I am not sufficiently knowledgeable to pass judgement on it, Gerald then moves on to what is probably complete fantasy in linking the Little People with the witches. He seems to be suggesting that the Little People were the heath dwellers, or "heathens", and that they were associated with much anti-clerical activity, including the Robin Hood legend, the May Games and sabbats attended by six thousand people! In the process they became known as witches.

Gerald saw certain similarities between the witches and the Knights Templar, such as wearing cords, the use of the chalice and the kiss at initiation. The one point where Gerald strongly emphasised the difference between the witches and the Templars was in who was able to initiate:

> The witches tell me: "The law always has been that power must be passed from man to woman or from woman to man ... (The reason is that great love is apt to occur between people who go through the rites together)." They go on to say: "The Templars broke this age-old rule and passed the power from man to man: this led to sin and in so doing it brought about their downfall." [*Witchcraft Today* – p69]

Gerald also drew attention to the similarity between the witches' rituals and the rites and myths of the Greek and Roman mysteries such as those of Dionysus, Orpheus and Eleusis. He emphasised the importance of the discovery of the Villa of the Mysteries in Pompeii, which he had visited in 1952, as previously the secrets were kept and never revealed. There are wall paintings, containing 29 figures. Gerald quotes Professor Vittorio Macchioro:

> It is evident that we have a single act divided into several episodes depicting the story of one draped female figure who

reappears in all the episodes. The story is a series of liturgical ceremonies by means of which the woman is initiated into the Orphic Mystery and attains communion with Zagreus. [*Witchcraft Today* – p85]

Gerald quotes Macchioro at length describing the story of the initiation into the mysteries as revealed in the wall paintings. He concludes:

I showed a picture of these frescoes to an English witch, who looked at it very attentively before saying: "So they knew the secret in those days." [*Witchcraft Today* – p88]

There is a rather unusual chapter entitled "Out of the Land of Egypt" which quotes Pennethorne Hughes:

Studies of the magic and ritual of Africa have in the last few years established with some certainty that all the systems for the disturbance of consciousness practised by the African Negro are derived from ancient Egypt. [*Witchcraft Today* – p93]

Gerald developed this idea somewhat and postulated that the European mystery cults had originated in Egypt and that the Voodoo practices, which he had studied when he was in New Orleans, were a mixture of European and African influences. I think Gerald was really trying to put forward what is known as diffusionism, although he also says that similar practices may have come into existence in different places independently of each other.

The chapter entitled "Irish Witchcraft" is really an amalgam of various seemingly unconnected items. Firstly, there is the story of Dame Alice Kyteler, accused of witchcraft in the 14th Century, which is taken from Margaret Murray's *The Witch Cult in Western Europe.* There is then an interesting account of a witch cult which was "practising nowadays", meeting in a quarry, holding full moon rituals, sacrificing animals to the moon, with a high priestess called Diana. What this was has never been determined and whether it continued, and if so for how long, I do not know.

I get the distinct impression that much of this material is just padding to eke out the relatively small amount of material he obtained from the witches. Much of it can now be challenged academically and consists of little more than Gerald's ideas of some incidents in the history of witchcraft.

Gerald always needed help in bringing a manuscript to the stage where it would be suitable for publication. He realised that he needed help with *New Light on Witchcraft* and I suspect that he approached his old friend Ross Nichols, who had acted as assistant editor for *The Occult Observer* and had also edited and revised a 19th Century French work, Paul Christian's *The History and Practice of Magic,* which was published in two volumes by the Forge Press in 1952.

Nichols took on the job enthusiastically and also approached Gerald Yorke, whom he had met through *The Occult Observer* and who worked for the well-respected publisher Rider and Co., which specialised in books on the occult and mysticism. Rider offered Gerald a contract and Nichols was appointed in 1953 to edit *New Light on Witchcraft* for publication. Francis King implies that Nichols' role was an important one in making the book what it is, when he writes:

> ... not at all a bad book, for the reader responsible for its acceptance, himself an occult scholar of distinction, managed to blue-pencil most of the more rubbishy passages. [Francis King – *Ritual Magic in England* – Neville Spearman 1970 p180]

It would certainly be interesting to see the original version, partly to check the rejected passages to see whether they were as "rubbishy" as King suggests, as I suspect that they may actually have contained some of the most interesting material.

I have in fact seen a typed annotated manuscript of an early version of *New Light on Witchcraft,* which differs to some extent from the final published version. In it, there is a passage which is very revealing of what Gerald got from his association with the witches:

> In my own case ... they well knew my views. I was intensely interested in the subject. I did not believe in their gods as such, but I believed in the change which we call death and in fertility, that biological urge which we see every day, and I loved the beauty of their stories, of the great spirits controlling these forces, and frankly enjoyed assisting at the rites in their honour ... [*New Light on Witchcraft* – pp42-43]

Gerald certainly seems to have been involved in quite a lot of negotiation about the draft manuscript, with Yorke on the one hand and with the witches on the other. Ross Nichols was also undoubtedly closely involved in the whole process. An indication of the matters which were covered in this negotiation is provided in a surviving letter from Gerald to Yorke. He had obviously submitted a draft of the manuscript for comment, which Yorke had made, and this was Gerald's response. The topics covered in the letter included yoga, a hallucinatory drug called soma, the Knights Templar and certain details of the witch rituals. Gerald had obviously included quite a lot about yoga, which Yorke had persuaded him to cut out, presumably because it was not directly relevant to the subject.

I am sure that there must have been other correspondence between Yorke and Gerald, although much may have been carried out indirectly via Nichols. One thing that changed was the title, almost certainly at the suggestion of the publishers, from *New Light on Witchcraft* to the more punchy and informative *Witchcraft Today*.

Margaret Murray agreed to write the foreword to the book. Gerald had known her since before the war and was certainly well aware of her work on witchcraft. He usually called the Craft "the witch cult" following her usage of the term in her book, *The Witch-Cult in Western Europe* (Oxford 1921).

Witchcraft Today was published in November 1954. It sold well, Gerald Gardner's first book to do so, and it made his name. The difference was that for the first time he had not paid the costs of production. Moreover, a mainstream publisher such as Rider had a good distribution system, which is always a key ingredient in sales figures. Gerald Yorke, writing in April 1958, noted that the book had sold more than 5,500 copies.

It certainly achieved reviews in several of the journals of the organisations of which Gerald was a member. These reviews were rather dismissive. That in *Folk-Lore* is unsigned and refers to the book as "an apology for witchcraft" and considers that it "can hardly be regarded as a serious contribution to a very complex and highly controversial subject". The reviewer for the *Journal of the Society for Psychical Research*, Geoffrey B. Riddehough, takes up this theme, saying, "Somehow, the apology is not quite convincing". Despite the adverse reviews, the book has been included in the permanent collections of most major public libraries in Britain and throughout the world, and for a generation was likely to have been an enquirer's first taste of the subject. It is still, for many, a classic text.

Philip Heselton is a well-known writer on Wicca, Paganism and Earth mysteries. He is the author of *Wiccan Roots: Gerald Gardner and the Modern Witchcraft Revival* and the two-volume *Witchfather: A Life of Gerald Gardner*.

The Evolution of Alexandrian Witchcraft

Frances Billinghurst

I had to do something because I couldn't refuse. I couldn't refuse because no one else in the world could do what I could do and a job had to be done. (Alex Sanders, 1986)[1]

The Alexandrian tradition of witchcraft evolved out of Gardnerian witchcraft during the early 1960s, the decade of social change and freedom of expression, and refers to a style of witchcraft that was instigated by Orrell Alexander Carter, better known as Alex Sanders. As such, it is impossible to talk about the tradition without first providing insight into the man himself.

Born on 6 June 1926 in Birkenhead, England (near Liverpool), Sanders was introduced to esoteric thought early in his childhood by his mother and maternal grandmother, Mary Bibby[2], hereditary Welsh witch who was allegedly a descendant of the Welsh chieftain Owain Glyndŵr, the "last king of the witches".[3] It was his grandmother, as Sanders informed reporter June Jones, who initiated him at the age of seven in an act that allegedly involved nicking his scrotum, which he described as being a "pale replica" of the act once carried out in Sparta where males were emasculated in order to become priests of the Moon Goddess.[4] This rather controversial story of initiation Sanders defended up until his death, despite disbelief by even some of his own initiates.

A gifted psychic, Sanders worked within spiritualist churches and by the late 1940s had become a renowned psychic medium as well as a healer; one of his better known cures being that performed on his daughter, Janice, who was born with a twisted left foot, which he corrected through the use of warm olive oil.[5] It was as a psychic medium that Sanders was first introduced to

Maxine Morris by her own mother.[6] In 1965 the couple were joined in a documented "witch's marriage" (handfasting), with the union being legalised in 1968, and resulting in two children, Maya and Victor. Although Sanders and Maxine ended their relationship in 1971, it was not until 1982 that they actually divorced.

Since his death from lung cancer on 30 April 1988, Sanders still appears to be either loved or loathed by those he taught as well as those who did not resonate with his bisexual lifestyle, the magic he produced, or his means in making the Craft more accessible. Highly respected Gardnerian High Priestess and "mother" of Gardnerian Witchcraft, Doreen Valiente, described Sanders as someone who "...gets ideas that are for things we ought to be doing. Perhaps that is why the powers that be allow him to carry on so long, to keep us on our toes".[7]

Sanders' attempts to make the Craft more accessible to those who sought initiation into its Mysteries and to educate the public about its practices saw him labelled as an oath breaker and an exhibitionist, who allowed the media to attend his coven's rituals, resulting in images of naked witches being splashed across the newspapers. Author Ronald Hutton acknowledges that, in doing so, Sanders however managed a rather remarkable achievement of taking on the sensationalist press of the time and defeating it.[8] Sanders' critics were not as kind. Possibly as a form of distancing themselves from the publicity, it was rumoured that Sanders was never properly initiated and that he stole the Gardnerian *Book of Shadows*,[9] thus indicating that he was a fraud. This hearsay continues today, contrary to proof indicating that Sanders was in fact properly initiated and therefore obtained the *Book of Shadows* via valid means.[10]

Despite some 25 years having passed since his death, Sanders is still often criticised as being an egotistical showman who turned witchcraft into a laughing stock with his public antics.[11] Due to his mischievous streak, it is difficult to ascertain whether what was made available to the media was something Sanders had constructed as bona fide Alexandrian Craft or part of a show. Unfortunately, it is easier to believe the latter as a form of self-preservation that developed into "desperate monomania".[12]

To his admirers, however, Sanders was a "Pagan magi"[13] and someone who was "extremely generous"[14] when it came to not only sharing his occult knowledge, but also whatever else he owned. Often critical of Sanders, Alexandrian initiate and author Janet Farrar confirmed that he refused to withhold the Mysteries from anyone as he personally believed the knowledge was for sharing.[15] He was also described as having "done more to clear the air on the subject of modern Wicca and put it into perspective than anyone in this country"[16] and his "gift to us all who knew him was his deep love for the Craft",[17] from which inspiration can be drawn from.

Sanders' generous nature made him extremely gullible, so much so that, despite initiating hundreds, if not thousands, into his tradition of witchcraft, when he died at St Helen's Hospital in Hastings, England, he died alone.

Such was Sanders' extremely controversial way of bringing witchcraft into the public arena that even when he made a public apology for his many "stupidities", [18] these have remained the focus of his legacy as opposed to his more positive contributions to the evolution of Gardnerian witchcraft, of which there were three notable additions: the admittance of gay and bisexual men; the inclusion of ceremonial magic; and the training of initiates that extended around the world.

In a way, Sanders acknowledged the extent of the web of Mystery and illusion he had created when, in the preface to *A Coin for the Ferryman*, it states: "If I told you the truth, you wouldn't believe me. That is, of course, if you understand me in the first place which is rather doubtful. If you did, you may send yourself mad."[19]

King of the Witches

Ever since the release of Jones' book, the title *King of the Witches* has been misinterpreted as being one that Sanders claimed for his own self. Instead, it was bestowed upon him in 1965 by the leaders of 12 covens that had branched off from his original Manchester group. This title was one that both Jones[20] and Maxine[21] state Sanders reluctantly "accepted with much humility and reluctance"[22] despite his later renowned egotistical behaviour and use of the title.

The title was also never intended to refer to Sanders as being the "king" of all witches, including non-Gardnerian traditions. It was an honorary title that referred to his position of authority and leadership over his own tradition of Wytchcraft and, as Galatea advises, any power that Sanders had was his ability to instil into the initiate their own ability to learn for themselves.[23] Some people have questioned whether Sanders actually did rule over such a larger number of covens. Maxine has advised that when she initiated in 1964, a number of covens had already branched off from the Manchester one that he ran with Sylvia Tatham,[24] and that the very nature of the training and initiation undertaken actually encouraged the formation of covens.

Shortly after his death in 1988, the Council of Elders of the Alexandrian tradition released a statement declaring that according to the Law of the Craft, a "king" was only chosen whenever the need arose, and that after due consideration, an unanimous motion was determined that there was no need for the position to be filled. The Council went on to state that, "Alex Sanders led the Hidden Children of the Goddess into the light. It was a task well done and it was his last and most earnest wish that they should continue their work into the light."[25] The Council has never convened since.

Alexandrian Tradition of Witchcraft

The name describing the style of witchcraft taught by Sanders was first recorded in Stewart Farrar's 1970 book, *What Witches Do*,[26] and as such was originally believed to have been a term coined by Farrar. In the 2010 reprint of this book, however, the term "Alexandrian" seems to have originated from an interview where Sanders was quoted as saying "those [witches] that don't want publicity tend to refer to my witches as 'Alexandrians'."[27] Another popular origin is that the term referred to the ancient Egyptian city of Alexandria that once housed the famous library built by Alexander the Great. In naming the tradition after the great library, Sanders believed that "these great ideals of furthering knowledge and understanding could continue".[28] Regardless of its origins, the name stuck, distinguishing the then difference between Gardnerian and Alexandrian initiates.

Having originated out of Gardnerian witchcraft, the Alexandrian tradition has retained a number of similarities, one being the belief that "only a witch can make another witch"[29] and that this is achieved through the process of cross-gender initiation, of which there are three degrees. The act of initiation continues to be an important part of the Alexandrian tradition for it is the process that takes the initiate "through spiritual transformation and rebirths us as children of the Goddess"[30], something that is not possible via solitary means. There is no "self-initiation" within the Alexandrian tradition of witchcraft. Every ritual performed is participatory whereby the covener must be "properly prepared" and ready to engage fully in the work ahead. The focus of the coven is matriarchal, whereby the High Priestess is considered "first among equals"[31], an earthly representative of the Goddess. As such, her word on all coven matters is final and traditionally was considered "law", a form of "benevolent dictatorship",[32] something that does not appeal to everyone. The honouring of lunar rites and observation of the eight sabbats are also similar practices between the two traditions.

Despite his initiation into Gardnerian witchcraft, Sanders'

interest in what Gardner classified as "high magic" (that being the Qabalah and ceremonial magic) resulted in it being one of the more noticeable differences between the two traditions. Sanders is recorded as having taught magic as well as witchcraft to his initiates, and when the two are combined, according to Mary Rands, they complement each other, like "hand in glove".[33] Up until the late 1970s, it was actually important for the initiate to be able to perform a number of rituals that formed part of the Golden Dawn's Adeptus Minor grade. These included the Lesser Banishing Ritual of the Pentagram, the Middle Pillar, and the Rose Cross ritual.[34] This high magical influence later evolved into the "Ordine Della Luna in Constantinople" that Sanders later developed as an ancillary to the Alexandrian tradition and also included works based on other occultists such as that of Madeline Montalban. Sanders further placed an emphasis on the study of magical techniques such as clairvoyance, astral projection and thought transference as well as the use of charms and talismans.[35]

Today, the use of high magic may not be taught in all Alexandrian covens, and as a result of sharing and reconstituting between the Gardnerian and Alexandrian traditions, some lineages have dropped the emphasis on high magic in favour of becoming more analogous to Gardnerian witchcraft.[36] It was these "ancient ritual techniques"[37] that Sanders saw little benefit in passing on. Instead, he added his own experimental work as he was of the opinion that the Craft needed to continue evolving otherwise it would become stale. This, however, has been interpreted by some initiates as only being able to evolve within finite boundaries, resulting in more "progressive" lines often being deemed as "not Craft-like", especially those that retain the inclusion of high magic.

Due to Sanders' ongoing experimentation with magic, there is no one Alexandrian *Book of Shadows*. What is actually handed to the initiate is often described as a "starting point", containing the common core of basic rituals and information for the initiate to base their workings upon and to later expand upon. Janet Farrar has been critical as to how "unprepared" she and Stewart felt when they started their own coven and, in particular, later in 1975 when they moved to Ireland.[38] This may have been because Sanders had his own goal and vision with respect to his own work and that in providing only the basics, this could only encourage his initiates to seek the same investigation. Whatever the truth, it will never truly be known.

As the popularity of the books published by Janet and Stewart Farrar grew, so did a number of misconceptions, the main one being that the material contained within *What Witches Do* and *Eight Sabbats for Witches* was that of the Alexandrian *Book of Shadows*. Whilst versions of Gardner's *Book of Shadows* may have found their way into the public domain (the validity of which is often disputed by Gardnerian initiates), there is still no true publically accessible copy of the Alexandrian *Book of Shadows* (for reasons given above). Another misconception is that the Oak and Holly King cycle (as recorded in *Eight Sabbats for Witches*) formed part of the Alexandrian tradition. Despite numerous statements by the authors[39] as well as Elders of the tradition[40] advising to the contrary, these misconceptions continue today.

Over the years the term "Wicca" has been adapted to refer to modern styles of witchcraft that are based on Gardnerian and Alexandrian traditions. This is despite the fact that Sanders, Maxine, and even Gardner referred to themselves as "witches", the "Hidden Children of the Goddess" and "of the Wica". The term "Wiccan", used in this sense, is believed to have originated from an article that appeared in *Light* magazine in 1958 by Charles Cardell, an alleged hereditary witch who developed a dislike for Gardner. As such, he described Gardner's followers as "Wiccen" [sic] in an attempt to distinguish between the practices.[41] It is not clear when the use of "Wiccan" came into general usage referring to Gardnerian and Alexandrian witch-craft. In light of the increasing number of non-initiated modern

Pagans describing to their own practices as "Wiccan", the word is becoming synonymous with non-Gardnerian-styled modern Paganism in general.

A further noticeable change occurred sometime during the 1970s when Gardnerian and Alexandrian witchcraft changed from "a magically based religion into a nature based neo-Pagan one concerned with environmental matters ... and the legal rights of its followers."[42] As such, today the Alexandrian tradition of witchcraft is often described as being an "oathbound, magic-using Pagan Mystery priesthood"[43] with ancient roots originating in the British Isles"[44] formalised in the 20th century by Gerald Gardner, as opposed to a "Mystery cult" that it was once referred to as being.

The Tradition Down Under

Having spread around the globe, one of the better known influences of Alexandrian witchcraft within Australia was Ian Watts (more commonly known as Simon Goodman) who was given a charter by the Council of Alexandrian Elders to initiate witches in the lands south of the equator. Goodman's relationship with Sanders appears to have been somewhat tumultuous as, in a letter dated 5 September 1983, Sanders accused Goodman of promoting a "Pickingsgill Disitation"[45] [sic] which he found to be "very tripe"[46] and which Sanders considered to be "not the way of the Mother".[47] Despite this, Goodman allegedly composed an obituary in 1988 stating that Sanders "was always ready to pass on the extensive information learned in his years of Craft practice. A warm, sincere and generous and giving man, he was ever ready to give freely of himself and to share with the many people who sought him out".[48]

Goodman himself was instrumental within the Australian occult scene during the 1970s, being a catalyst for the formation of a number of groups (including the "Covanentus Quercus"), Pagan festivals and even the Occult Reference Centre (based in

Canberra). He passed through the veil prematurely on 23 September 1991 (the Spring Equinox in the Southern Hemisphere) at the age of 40.[49]

Taking a Northern Hemispheric and largely British focused priesthood south of the equator resulted in a number of issues for Southern Hemispheric initiates that still arise today. Some lineages have felt a desire to keep "true" to the original *Book of Shadows* handed to them, resulting in the observation of dates being in contrast to the actual seasons as occurring in the Southern Hemisphere. Ongoing debates further arise over the placement of elemental representations as well as the direction a circle should be cast – either to keep with the original Northern Hemispheric egregore or to work with the energetic flow of the land. Following her visit to Australia in 2008, British HPS Vivianne Crowley comment that she "... found it impossible to cast a clockwise circle in Australia and to me the flow of power seemed to be definitely anticlockwise, the Australian direction of the sun".[50] This statement summoned up what Southern Hemispheric initiates, this writer included, have been saying for ages: due to the difference in the energy currents, it is impossible to follow the original *Book of Shadows* with respect to circle casting and elemental placement. As such, within a number of Southern Hemispheric lineages, the Alexandrian tradition of witchcraft has evolved to include various aspects that are more pertinent to practitioners residing south of the equator.

While Sanders stated that the Craft needs to evolve otherwise it will become stagnant, any additions made to the original *Book of Shadows* are done under strict guidelines to ensure that the "essence" of the tradition is still reflected. This motive becomes more pertinent when more facts are revealed. While both Gardner and Sanders once instructed their initiates that their forms of witchcraft were an ancient practice, most initiates today acknowledge that it is in fact a relatively new religion that consists of practices cobbled together from various sources based on alleged ancient beliefs and practices.

Frater Barrabbas considers that "preservation is nothing more than an historical exercise"[51] as witchcraft continues to grow in order to become a more mature religious tradition. As such, this is hardly a negative thing as where would any spiritual religious tradition be "if it never required the invention or borrowing of lore from any other sources?"[52] Regardless of whether a lineage evolves its tradition of witchcraft or keeps true to the original *Book of Shadows*, what is important is that witchcraft offers an authentic portal into the Mysteries of life and death, of light and darkness, and of the spiritual evolution of all living things.[53]

What Sanders presented to the world in the 1960s was a new powerful version of witchcraft that was deeply rooted in magic, and a tradition that challenged its initiates with its various disciplines. The rituals and liturgy are the core of the Alexandrian tradition as their objective is to unlock the doors to the Mysteries and reveal secret lore that cannot be written down. This is, after all, the underlying spirit of witchcraft itself for it contains the inner truths that can only be rediscovered via this method and, as such, means that each witch will have their own perspective on these Mysteries. What the tradition does is provide a set of keys to assist in the easier identification of these Mysteries. Over time as a tradition progresses and develops, what occurs is that the depth of these Mysteries is obtained, as well as an ever evolving egregore being tapped into.

Despite the personal failings that Alex Sanders is known for, his greatest legacy is that the tradition of witchcraft he exposed the world to in the 1960s continues to evolve, allowing more initiates to access the Mysteries and to share his passion.

Frances Billinghurst is an initiated witch and High Priestess of an active coven based in Adelaide, South Australia and author of *Dancing the Sacred Wheel: A Journey through the Southern Sabbats*.

References

D'Este, Sorita and Rankine, David, *Wicca Magickal Beginnings: A Study of the Possible Origins of the Rituals and Practices Found in this Modern Tradition of Pagan Witchcraft and Magick* (Avalonia, 2008)

Di Fiosa, Jimahl, *A Coin for the Ferryman: The Death and Life of Alex Sanders* (Createspace, 2010)

Di Fiosa, Jimahl, *A Voice in the Forest: Spirit Conversations with Alex Sanders* (Harvest Shadows Publications, 2004 (Harvest, 2002)

Di Fiosa, Jimahl, *All the King's Children* (Createspace, 2010)

Farrar, Stewart, *What Witches Do: A Modern Coven Revealed* (Peter Davis, 1971)

Howard, Michael, *Modern Wicca: A History from Gerald Gardner to the Present* (Llewellyn, 2009)

Hutton, Ronald, *The Triumph of the Moon: A History of Modern Pagan Witchcraft* (Oxford University Press, 2001)

Jones, June, *King of the Witches: The World of Alex Sanders* (Pan Books, 1971)

Sanders, Maxine, *Maxine: The Witch Queen* (Wyndham Publications, 1976)

Sanders, Maxine, *Firechild: The Life and Magic of Maxine Sanders "Witch Queen"* (Mandrake Books, 2007)

Endnotes

1. Di Fiosa, Jimahl, *A Coin for the Ferryman: The Death and Life of Alex Sanders* (Createspace, 2010)
2. Sanders, Maxine, *Firechild: The Life and Magic of Maxine Sanders "Witch Queen"* (Mandrake Books, 2007)
3. Jones, June, *King of the Witches: The World of Alex Sanders* (Pan Books, 1971)
4. ibid
5. Jones, June, *King of the Witches: The World of Alex Sanders* (Pan Books, 1971)

6. Sanders, Maxine, *Firechild: The Life and Magic of Maxine Sanders "Witch Queen"* (Mandrake Books, 2007)

7. Letter by Doreen Valiente to John Score dated 13 October 1971 as recorded in *A Coin for the Ferryman* by Jimahl di Fosa

8. ibid

9. Such accusations were made by Gardnerian High Priestesses, Patricia Crowther and Eleanor Bone, as well as John Score, editor of *Light* magazine. (Howard, Michael, *Modern Wicca: A History from Gerald Gardner to the Present* (Llewellyn, 2009)

10. Both Maxine Sanders and Ronald Hutton refer to a letter dated 5 September 1963 from Pat Kopanski (an ex-initiate of Pat Crowther) to Gerald Gardner advising that Sanders had received his First Degree initiation in Medea's coven on 9 March 1963. Due to subsequent events, Kopanski (as Second Degree) elevated Sanders whereas Tatham received her Third Degree from "Loic", the husband of Monique Wilson (a High Priestess of Gardner's). After Kopanski left the coven, Tatham elevated Sanders to Third Degree and it is through Tatham's connection with Monique Wilson that Sanders is believed to have received the Gardnerian *Book of Shadows*. (http://bissekart.zoomshare.com/files/pickingill/1.html)

11. Hutton, Ronald, *The Triumph of the Moon: A History of Modern Pagan Witchcraft* (Oxford University Press, 2001)

12. Sanders, Maxine, *Firechild: The Life and Magic of Maxine Sanders "Witch Queen"* (Mandrake Books, 2007).

13. Tiresius, Frater Barrabbas, *Advanced Alexandrian Wicca* (http://fraterbarrabbas.blogspot.com.au)

14. Sanders, Maxine, *Firechild: The Life and Magic of Maxine Sanders "Witch Queen"* (Mandrake Books, 2007)

15. Di Fiosa, Jimahl, *A Coin for the Ferryman: The Death and Life of Alex Sanders* (Createspace, 2010)

16. Farrar, Stewart, *What Witches Do: A Modern Coven Revealed*

(Peter Davis, 1971)

17. A comment by made Alexandrian initiate, Nigel, as recorded in *A Coin for the Ferryman: The Death and Life of Alex Sanders* by Jinahl Di Fiosa

18. An open letter entitled "Many Paths of Wicca" that appeared in *The Cauldron* (Lammas 1979)

19. Alex Sanders (October 1986) as recorded in *A Coin for the Ferryman: The Death and Life of Alex Sanders* by Jimahl di Fosa (Createspace, 2010)

20. Jones, June, *King of the Witches: The World of Alex Sanders* (Pan Books, 1971)

21. Sanders, Maxine, *Firechild: The Life and Magic of Maxine Sanders "Witch Queen"* (Mandrake Books, 2007)

22. ibid

23. Di Fiosa, Jimahl, *A Coin for the Ferryman: The Death and Life of Alex Sanders* (Createspace, 2010)

24. Sanders, Maxine, *Firechild: The Life and Magic of Maxine Sanders "Witch Queen"* (Mandrake Books, 2007)

25. Witches' Voice, *The Alexandrian Tradition* (http://www.witchvox.com/va/dt_va.html?a=cabc&c=trads&id=15046)

26. Sanders, Maxine, *Firechild: The Life and Magic of Maxine Sanders "Witch Queen"* (Mandrake Books, 2007))

27. Witches' Voice, *The Alexandrian Tradition* (http://www.witchvox.com/va/dt_va.html?a=cabc&c=trads&id=15046)

28. The Wellhead (http://www.thewellhead.org.uk)

29. The Wellhead, *An Introduction to Alexandrian Wicca* (http://www.thewellhead.org.uk/tradition/an-introduction-to-alexandr.html)

30. ibid

31. Witches' Voice, *The Alexandrian Tradition* (http://www.witchvox.com/va/dt_va.html?a=cabc&c=trads&id=15046)

32. ibid

33. Di Fiosa, Jimahl, *A Coin for the Ferryman: The Death and Life of Alex Sanders* (Createspace, 2010)

34. Tiresius, Frater Barrabbas, *Advanced Alexandrian Wicca* (http://fraterbarrabbas.blogspot.com.au)
35. Hutton, Ronald, *The Triumph of the Moon: A History of Modern Pagan Witchcraft* (Oxford University Press, 2001)
36. Tiresius, Frater Barrabbas, *Advanced Alexandrian Wicca* (http://fraterbarrabbas.blogspot.com.au)
37. Jones, June, *King of the Witches: The World of Alex Sanders* (Pan Books, 1971)
38. Di Fiosa, Jimahl, *A Coin for the Ferryman: The Death and Life of Alex Sanders* (Createspace, 2010)
39. Farrar, Janet, and Farrar, Stewart, *Our Wiccan Origins* (http://www.wicca.utvinternet.com/origins.htm)
40. Witches' Voice, *The Alexandrian Tradition* (http://www.witchvox.com/va/dt_va.html?a=cabc&c=trads&id=15046)
41. d'Este, Sorita and Rankine, David, *Wicca Magickal Beginnings: A Study of the Possible Origins of the Rituals and Practices Found in this Modern Tradition of Pagan Witchcraft and Magick* (Avalonia, 2008)
42. Howard, Michael, *Modern Wicca: A History from Gerald Gardner to the Present* (Llewellyn, 2009)
43. The Wellhead, *An Introduction to Alexandrian Wicca* (http://www.thewellhead.org.uk/tradition/an-introduction-to-alexandr.html)
44. Howard, Michael, *Modern Wicca: A History from Gerald Gardner to the Present* (Llewellyn, 2009)
45. Letter to Simon Goodman dated 5 September 1983
46. ibid
47. ibid
48. Boucca Society (http://webspace.webring.com/people/ub/boucca_society/simongoodman.html)
49. ibid
50. Howard, Michael, *Modern Wicca: A History from Gerald Gardner to the Present* (Llewellyn, 2009)
51. Tiresius, Frater Barrabbas, *Advanced Alexandrian Wicca*

(http://fraterbarrabbas.blogspot.com.au)
52. ibid
53. ibid

The Seax Tradition

Alaric Albertsson

When it was first published in 1974, Raymond Buckland's *The Tree: The Complete Book of Saxon Witchcraft* introduced a new tradition and influenced the future of Wicca throughout the world.

Buckland was a young Englishman already in his twenties when Gerald Gardner published *Witchcraft Today* and, later, *The Meaning of Witchcraft*. Despite this, Buckland did not learn of Wicca until after he moved to America with his first wife, Rosemary, in 1962. Drawn to the Wiccan religion, the Bucklands traveled to Perth, Scotland, a year later, where they were initiated by Gardner's high priestess, Monique Wilson. Gardner and Buckland had become friends by that time and Buckland soon became Gardner's spokesperson in America.

While there were other forms of witchcraft practiced in the 1960s, it was Wicca that most often caught the public's attention. At that time Wicca was a purely initiatory path notable for its nature-worship, elements of ceremonial magic and its ritual nudity. The religion had a strict hierarchical structure.

Because of the initiation process, Wicca could only grow slowly and, as such, was inaccessible to many people. Even after receiving an initiation, a Wiccan could have his or her credibility revoked by someone higher up the initiatory line. By the early 1970s, Buckland felt a need for something with less of a despotic power structure.

There was nothing unique about creating a new tradition even then. In 1957, Doreen Valiente had broken away from Gerald Gardner's coven to form her own, eschewing Gardner's "old laws of the Craft". Alex Sanders was another Englishman initiated roughly the same time as Buckland; by the mid-1960s he had modified the Gardnerian rituals to create his own Alexandrian tradition. The difference was that these others retained the essential hierarchy and organization of Gardner's tradition, whereas Buckland was creating something novel with his Seax Wica tradition.

"I created it simply for the use of myself and a few friends," says Buckland. "It was only when word got out (as it always does in Pagan circles!) as to what I was doing that I found there was a much greater interest."

Seax Wica went public in the Yule 1973 issue of a national Pagan periodical called *Earth Religion News*, only months before its rituals and philosophy were published by Weiser Books as *The Tree: The Complete Book of Saxon Witchcraft*.

The lineage of Seax Wica can be seen in its name. While almost all Wiccans today still pronounce the word as WICK-eh (rather than using the Old English pronunciation WITCH-eh), the overwhelming majority now use the Old English "cc" spelling (Wicca). Gardner only occasionally used the word Wica in his writing, and then always with a single "c" spelling, possibly because, as Buckland says, "he was notoriously dyslexic and not the most accurate researcher". So why was the Seax tradition dubbed Seax Wica with the single "c" spelling? Buckland tells me, "Since that was the form (Gardner) adopted and kept throughout his books, I followed suit, as an early devotee of Gardner." This spelling continues to be popular among many followers of the tradition, not because of ignorance, but from pride in their history.

Buckland has received some unwarranted criticism from people who do not understand what Seax Wica is. In *The Tree* (titled in a later edition as *Buckland's Book of Saxon Witchcraft*), Buckland does not claim to present the pre-Christian Saxon religion. Seax Wica is another expression of Wicca, pure and simple. "The Seax Wica was to be a new form, quite separate from my earlier association with the Gardnerian tradition," he says, "and I was not trying to reconstruct an original religion so I took the Saxon culture only as a bare skeleton on which to hang the rites and practices I devised." Thus the Lord and Lady of Seax Wica are the Saxon deities Woden and Freya (Fréo), initiated witches are known by the Saxon word gesith (meaning "companion"), and one of the officers of a Seax coven holds the Saxon title of Thegn. Even the name of the tradition itself, *Seax*, is a Saxon word for a large knife. (The knife, or athamé, is a primary working tool in Wicca.) Beyond this, Seax Wica bears very little resemblance to the religion of the pre-Christian Saxons. Some of the differences were intentional. For example, Buckland chose to pair Woden with Freya because he believed the name of Woden's actual consort, Frig, had a vulgar meaning in Modern English. (The word "frig", meaning to copulate or masturbate, was in more common usage in the 1970s than it is today.) Celtic names were used for some of the holidays, such as Lughnasadh rather than the Anglo-Saxon Hlafmæsse, simply because they were more familiar to the Wiccan community. Instead of her (historical) golden necklace, Freya has a "silver circlet" in the Seax tradition.

But the significant changes found in Seax Wica were unrelated to its cultural imagery; the important changes were in the very structure of the tradition.

A New Wicca

Until 1974, a person claiming to follow Wicca with no Gardnerian initiatory validation would often be regarded by other Wiccans with disdain. There were some exceptions, such as Zsuzsanna Budapest, who founded the Dianic Wicca tradition. But formal initiation rapidly became less important after the publication of *The Tree.* Buckland continued to advocate initiation. However, his new Seax Wica tradition offered a Rite of Self Dedication for those who could not find a coven. Now anyone could enter the Wiccan religion, and the person who had opened that door was none other than a man who had been initiated by Gerald Gardner's high priestess.

Behind closed doors many people were creating their own variants of Wicca, and they had the resources to do so. Lady Sheba had published her version of the coveted *Book of Shadows*, a book of prayers and rituals. Authors such as Paul Huson, Louise Huebner and Sybil Leek inspired their readers to explore non-Gardnerian expressions of Pagan spirituality and magic. Most of the new traditions bolstered themselves with faux initiatory lineages that inevitably led back to a dead grandmother, a long-lost acquaintance or some other person conveniently unavailable for questioning.

The Seax tradition cast aside the need for initiatory validation, and offered options previously unknown in Wicca. The Gardnerian-style power hierarchy was completely dismantled in Seax Wica. A Seax coven has a priest and priestess to facilitate the group's rituals, but these positions are elected annually rather than giving anyone a permanent, irrevocable seat of power. Whereas in the Gardnerian tradition the priestess must be present to conduct a coven meeting, in the Seax tradition either the priest or the priestess, or both, can convene a meeting. Whether initiated or self-dedicated, all gesiths enjoy the same status, and there is no degree system for higher levels of initiation.

These changes were specific to Seax Wica, but they had a ripple effect throughout the Wiccan religion. Of course there were still "old school" priestesses and priests who ruled their covens with iron fists, but these began to diminish in number. Wiccan leaders who abused their followers were more likely to see those followers leave for greener pastures. The religion of Wicca changed irrevocably, and today there are countless Wiccans who proudly admit that they have never been initiated and feel no compulsion to seek out any validation beyond what they have received from their Gods.

Seax Wica was also the first tradition to openly welcome gay men, even though Buckland himself did not think it likely that gays and lesbians would be attracted to Wicca due to its male-female dualism. In this he was mistaken.

A Worldwide Tradition

As it turned out, gay men *were* attracted to Wicca. Regardless of their sexual orientation, gay men had come into existence through the male-female unions of mothers and fathers. Like everybody else, they were sustained by food produced through male-female fertility. Gays were as much a part of the cycle of life celebrated by Wicca as their heterosexual brethren. (Lesbians, of course, were equally welcome in Seax Wica, but they also had another potential home in Budapest's Dianic tradition.)

People, straight *or* gay, who could not find other Wiccans were attracted by the Seax tradition's Rite of Self Dedication as well as the more open attitude towards solitary worship. Others were attracted to the egalitarian structure of Seax covens, and still others simply liked the Saxon trappings. For many reasons, people were drawn to a tradition that now has followers throughout the world.

As might be expected, Seax Wica tends to be more popular in countries with an Anglo-Saxon heritage such as the United Kingdom and the United States, but the tradition has a surprisingly extensive following in Peru. One coven in Peru, Meomer's Well, has members in the cities of Lima, Arequipa and Tacna. Juan Espinoza is a founder of the coven, which was established in 2001. He discovered Seax Wica in 1999 and discovered that "the form of the organization, the autonomy of the coven and fraternity with other Seax gesiths – coveners and solitaries – of other countries was amazing."

Like so many others who have been drawn to Seax Wica, Espinoza and the other coveners of Meomer's Well appreciate the freedom they have found in this tradition. Many groups adapt the official Seax rituals to their own needs, which is an acceptable practice in Seax Wica. For Meomer's Well, one change was to revere Woden's consort Frig. Since the coveners speak Spanish as their first language, the subtleties of English vulgarity are less relevant. They have added and adapted some other rituals and, like most Wiccans living south of the equator, have reversed the sabbats to correspond correctly to their seasonal changes.

In coming years Seax Wica may become more prevalent in other South American countries. Espinoza says that his coven "helps other groups of self-dedicated (gesiths) in Argentina, Bolivia and Chile." He also tells me that "people from the Philippines have asked us to guide them in the Seax Wica tradition."

A Personal Tradition

Since there is no practical means of enforcing conformity, Wiccans in many traditions other than Seax Wica have often been known to change the rituals and practices passed on to them. Buckland openly encourages this in the Seax tradition. "Humankind is forever changing; adapting and adopting," he says. "Religion is a very personal thing and should be comfortable for the practitioner. It would therefore be contradictory to produce a tradition that was set in stone and locked into hard and fast rules and guidelines."

Buckland worked hard to keep egotism and any ability for power building out of Seax Wica. The tradition does have three designations describing a person's involvement, but these are not ranks as such. Those initiated or self-dedicated into Seax Wica are known as gesiths. Those who intend to be initiated or self dedicated but are in the process of learning more about the tradition are referred to as ceorls. Finally, a person who is not involved in Seax Wica (basically everybody else) is a theow. Because these are descriptive rather than ranks, it is entirely

37

possible for a theow to take an interest in Seax Wica, thus becoming a ceorl, and then dedicate himself or herself to become a gesith all in the space of a few hours. (This would usually only happen, of course, if the theow was already familiar with Wicca.)

A Seax coven may and probably will require more before initiating a ceorl *into the coven*. Here again we see the freedom inherent in Seax Wica. Covens are intensely autonomous, answering to nobody. Each is free to expand its own rituals and practices. There is no national or international leadership; no Witch Kings or Witch Queens. Buckland himself is often called the *Fæder* of Seax Wica, but this is simply a respectful acknowledgment of his founding the tradition.

For a time Seax Wica had a Steward who people could go to with any questions about the tradition. In Buckland's own words:

> There were always questions to be answered. So when I could no longer find the necessary time I asked someone I knew – and had trained in the tradition – to take on that task. That was Michael Crow. He did an excellent job but eventually he, too, found himself in a similar position where he just didn't have time to devote to it. I therefore asked another person to take it on. Regrettably he had grossly misrepresented himself (or I had badly misjudged him) and did a lot of damage. I decided that the Seax Wica must sink or swim on its own merits. Hopefully I had given sufficient information to create a good foundation, and others could build from there. So there is no longer a Steward of the Seax Wica.

Even within Seax covens there is little "power" other than what priests and priestesses command through respect for their own deeds. The priest and priestess are both chosen by their fellow gesiths (coveners) to facilitate the group's rituals for at least one year. At the end of the year they may be asked to continue for another year, or the coven may vote for a new priest or priestess.

A Seax priest or priestess who has led a coven for two or more years, whether or not the years were consecutive, is known as a high priest or high priestess, but even this person has no permanent position of authority in the coven.

The freedom inherent in Seax Wica extends to the tradition's theology as well as its rituals and coven structure. As with most Wiccan traditions, and certainly all that descended from Gerald Gardner's construct, there is a focus on duality in worship – a reverence for a Lord and Lady – but how this Divine Pair is perceived can vary from one gesith to another, from one Seax coven to the next. Some believe the Wiccan Lord and Lady to be the entirety of divinity, with the Lord being a manifestation of all male deities and the Lady a manifestation of all female deities. This idea was summed up by Mary Violet Firth (a.k.a. Dion Fortune) in her novel *The Sea Priestess*, when she wrote, "All gods are one god, and all goddesses are one goddess."

On the other hand, Seax Wica accepts as equally valid the view that the Lord and Lady are but two among many deities. Historically the Saxons certainly acknowledged an array of gods and goddesses. Even the question of *which* Saxon deities should be revered is a personal choice for the Seax gesith. The god Woden usually takes the role of the Lord and Freya is very often the Lady, but in his introduction to *Buckland's Book of Saxon Witchcraft*, the Fæder of Seax Wica has said himself that any deities can be revered so long as they are Saxon deities.

Woden and Freya

Regardless of this freedom, the majority who follow Seax Wica do call upon Woden and Freya in their rituals. Woden is the chief of the Anglo-Saxon pantheon, a god of wisdom and magic. Freya is the Norse name of the goddess of passion and prosperity. In Old English her name would be rendered as Fréo, but in the Seax tradition her Norse name is almost always used.

From the very beginning Buckland was always open about

why he chose to name Freya as the Lady of Seax Wica rather than Woden's consort Frig (or Frige). In Modern English slang, the word "frig" is a vulgar term. But could the gods themselves have inspired Buckland on some unconscious level to substitute Freya for Frig? If we look only at the relationships between various Anglo-Saxon deities the pairing of Woden and Freya may seem awkward, but if we look at the *functions* of these deities the arrangement makes perfect sense. Magic has an inherent role in the practice of Seax Wica, as it does in most Wiccan traditions, and Woden and Freya are the two Anglo-Saxon deities most closely associated with the arcane arts. Woden is the wizard-god who gave mankind the mysteries of the runes. In addition to rune magic, Woden is called upon in an old Anglo-Saxon incantation known as the Nine Herbs Charm to promote healing with mystical powers. The goddess Freya (or Fréo) is the mistress of the magic of ecstatic trance. In the Ynglinga saga Freya teaches her magical arts to Odin (the Norse name for Woden). It makes sense that anyone following an Anglo-Saxon path would naturally call on these deities – Woden and Freya – for aid and counsel in magic.

Seax Wica Today

With covens and practitioners all over the globe, it is unlikely that the Seax tradition will fade away. With its rituals reprinted more than thirty years after *The Tree* was first published, the tradition continues to attract new followers, which it readily accommodates without the constraints of cumbersome initiation requirements. Anyone with access to the rituals can perform a self-dedication and begin worshipping the old gods.

Seax Wica has been a springboard inspiring many people to explore Anglo-Saxon spirituality. New Anglo-Saxon spiritual movements have arisen in both the United States and the United Kingdom, often under the leadership of former Seax gesiths such as Sean Percival, who founded the Lyblác tradition of

Anglo-Saxon Witchcraft. The Seax tradition has also inspired others such as myself. I was introduced to Anglo-Saxon deities several years before *The Tree* was published, but it would be less than honest to say that Buckland's tradition did not arouse me to focus on those deities and indigenous English spirituality.

Other people, of course, become gesiths of the Seax tradition – either through initiation or self-dedication – and remain so. When needed, they adapt the rituals or rewrite them entirely if necessary, infusing new life into a living, adaptable spiritual path. Espinoza says, "Seax Wica is not based on the orthopraxis of *The Tree*; it is in the experiences and reasoning of (the) gesiths that it grows."

For those experiences and reasoning, Seax Wica is likely to be around for a very long time.

Alaric Albertsson is a native of Missouri, but currently lives in western Pennsylvania. He is the author of *Travels Through Middle Earth: The Path of a Saxon Pagan*, *Wyrdworking: The Path of a Saxon Sorcerer* and *To Walk a Pagan Path: Practical Spirituality for Every Day*.

Eclectic Wicca

Dorothy Abrams

These days the people I know well who follow a Wiccan path are eclectic free spirits. They seek no permission for their practices. They direct their own journeys. They flee from any hint of authority. They mix and match ritual forms and pantheons to suit themselves. When a magical incantation rings false or awkward, they tend to throw it out. Our spiritual work has an opportunity to maintain a fresh energy about it. We can change quickly to keep our rituals original. Creativity becomes part of our spiritual practice. The words of Doreen Valiente are beautiful examples of Wiccan creativity. We use them once in a while. Twice in a while we write our own. Sometimes that feels like our Goddesses write pretty words through us. As eclectics, we are intimates of the deities. They are especially appreciated when the ritualist scheduled to lead a sabbat has an emergency, can't be at circle and didn't write a program. More than once we have created magic on the spot, just because we knew how. In my opinion, spontaneous events pack a wallop when they are grounded in a solid Pagan education in relationship with the Divine.

As a result of our spontaneity, eclectic Wiccans like myself can be criticized for "making it up as they go along." Sometimes we are judged to be fluffy bunny witches who fail to understand the power and responsibility that Wicca and other witchcraft traditions hold dear. Others may turn up their noses at New Age practices that have crept in under the hems of our robes: things like chakra clearings and channeling. Judgments of cultural appropriation can stick to us because we borrow freely from Eastern mysticism, shamanic practices, and African or Native American lore. I heard Raven Grimassi explain once that when he started out in the Strega tradition in the 1970s, all the witches had a common base of knowledge and tradition. In contrast, 21st century witches have branched out and changed their practices. One must define terms and watch carefully to see if the commonality we assume is real or not.

I am the co-founder of an eclectic group grounded in witchcraft and a Wiccan Pagan education. Ours is called the Web PATH Center, PATH standing for Pagan Academy of Teaching and Healing. We are an intentional community, though not one that lives collectively. We are committed to training ourselves and each other in what we have learned and experienced. In addition to teaching and healing each other, we believe creativity and the arts are an important part of Paganism. We have visual artists, musicians, writers, storytellers, crafters, herbalists, and others who bring the ecstasy of spirit into our rituals and our daily lives through their art. Many of us are self-taught. We encourage creativity of spirit and excellence, but do not limit such things to people who studied fine arts in school. People who thought they were not creative have found a wide river of originality running through them in exciting ways. In fact, I believe the ecstasy of spirit found in ritual, the Great Rite, and transformative meditation is the same rush we experience in creating artwork and in making love.

Like many other eclectic groups or individuals, The Web has consistency in the rituals we write. Some of our choices will resonate with other more traditional Wiccans. We cast a circle deosil for weaving energy together and building our community. We release it widdershins to unravel or release the spells we made. We ground every time we gather to celebrate the seasons and moons. We release the grounding when we are finished. We evoke the elementals and Guardians of the Watchtowers. We call the male and female deities together to balance polarity in the circle and ourselves. We draw down the moon. We walk the witches' mill as the Goddess speaks through us.

On the other hand, some of our practices are not resonant

with more traditional forms of Wicca. The Web has a patron Goddess in Grandmother Spider from the American Southwest indigenous traditions. However, we research the deities called for specific rituals from a variety of locations to make sure they are wise choices. They are likely from the same pantheon, though not always. We seek compatible masculine and feminine energy from those who wish to work magic with us on a sabbat or esbat. I believe they more often pick us than the other way around. Most of us experience the deities as individual spirit entities rather than archetypes of our ideation or cultural symbols. However, that is hardly a requirement.

We also recognize the Triple Goddess which may be Maiden, Mother, Crone or simply a trinity of ageless deities revealing different facets of personality or realms of authority. Gerald Gardner is assigned credit for this formation, but Virgil the Roman poet finds Hecate connected to three forms of Diana. Other ancients join Hecate to Selene of the moon, Artemis of the forest, and Persephone of the underworld. This naming of Hecate as three spirits is shamanic in my view, offering upper world, middle world and lower world guides. The Web weavings with the Goddesses and Gods is literal magic with spirit co-creators and in that we are eclectic rather than traditional.

Like many Wiccans, we work magic for the good of all and harm of none, emphasizing our strong ethical commitment to the greatest and highest blessings. We cite the Wiccan Rede and the rule of three as our basis for positive magic. We discourage negative workings like curses or hexes as carrying energy that could be a negative blow back on us individually or as a group. In addition, when we work magick, links are forged between the witches and the receiver. People we'd like to bind are not ones we'd like bound to us. Instead we create shields and wards to prevent interference from unwelcome sources.

The Web works healing in ritual and in our psychic network with Reiki, shamanism, chakras, meridians, auras, past lives, reflexology, sound and visualization. We have a healers list for intervention on behalf of our members, friends and family who ask for help. We withhold our hand if someone turns down our offer of help. People have the right of choice in magical healing as much as in medical healing. Healing under the auspices of the Web healers is free. Some of our healers also make their living in the healing arts and medical practice. Of course they have a right to charge their usual fees when they work on their own. The Web PATH Center has a broad base. Our roots run deep.

One of the teachers who helped develop *Wicca III: To Dare the Transformation* suggested that the practices at the Web were so diverse they confused people. Who are we? What do we really do? She is a close friend, sharer of my secrets, so I paid attention. How could we make our purpose clearer to people? Should we focus more narrowly on Wicca, since that is our first allegiance? After some deliberation most of us thought not. Welcoming people to join us in an open circle regardless of Pagan "denomination" enriches our knowledge. We learn more from diversity.

There is common sense in embracing diversity. Talking to people who agree with me tends to make me insular. Practicing Wicca with other like-minded Wiccans and no one else makes me stagnant. I need to be shaken up once in a while in order to ask why do I feel uncomfortable calling African Orishas as a white woman? What is there about a sweat lodge that warns me off? How do I think the integrity of a circle is compromised if it is worked earthwise instead of sunwise? As an honest intellectual and serious Pagan, I must be able to answer those questions in my own mind based on experience and connections with people. Otherwise I defend my own prejudices thinking they are the same thing as *truth*. The problem with exclusion of *the other* from a group is that I only speak with people who cannot challenge me sufficiently. In fact when working with other Gods and in other traditions, a circle has strength when it is made counter clockwise. A sweat lodge purifies the body and creates an openness to visions. The Orishas are approachable with proper respect by a person standing in her own power.

How is it we comfortably slide from one tradition to another? In honor of full disclosure, I am an Aries. There are several of us here in the Web. The Tower is my favorite tarot card. I embrace change and welcome a new slant on our routines. Not everyone is like that. I understand. I spent half a life time defending diversity in employment, housing and public accommodations. I spent another half a life time championing women's rights and human rights as an advocate and organizer. I can see the point of view of various people from many places around the circle. That comes from my academic studies and life experience. I would not expect to celebrate spirituality in a limited or conservative environment. Eclectic practice is made for me.

As a result of my history, and that of the Web's co-founders, the value we share at the Web is one of inclusion. We *want* to attract people from a variety of Pagan paths, ethnic backgrounds, sexual orientations, ages, skills and abilities. We have neo-Hellenists, people with Afro Cuban or Haitian training, Celtic, Norse, core shamanism, and New Age/Angel devotees sitting in circle together. We blend our beliefs into the web of universal consciousness. This is what we are named for – the connection woven by spirit and energy. Eclectic Wicca encourages us in piecing together a network of spirits and humans. Because we are an open circle, we never know which humans will attend, nor exactly what spirits come with them. Nevertheless we have never had a bad experience with this openness around the Wheel of the Year or the moon rituals.

What does our practice actually look like? The Web celebrates the eight sabbats, realizing the agrarian settlements may not have acknowledged all of them. We like the balance around the seasonal calendar of solstices and equinox celebrations with their cross quarters. We create ritual for the full moon which weaves the lunar connection with our spirits either in a formal drawing down or a similar meditative practice to bring the Goddess into our lives if not our bodies. We work magic with the full moon. We include the blade and chalice version of the Great Rite in several rituals, though not all of them. We offer initiations as people pass through the various stages of instruction. We use sacred drama for the Oak King/Holly King exchanges of pre-eminence when we have willing actors. None of those practices is required in Web ritual. All of them have been included as we consciously connect with the spiritual grid of power surrounding our planet.

In addition, any given ritual may embrace surprises. Our Samhain ritual includes mediumship and channeling. We teach how to use those inner senses and then practice them right in the circle. Our Yule ritual celebrates some sort of gift giving that involves psychic skills. For years we brought unwrapped presents to set out on a table, expecting each one to go to the intended celebrant, though the intention is of the spirit not the giver. Imbolc honors creativity with poetry, candle fire spells and knot magic. Spirits appear in the flames. Spring Equinox calls on fertility with egg spells. Beltane dances the May Pole as a fertility ritual, but results in trance drumming. Summer Solstice opens the Inner Court to a Hellenic God and Goddess channeled by the ritualists to answer questions in spontaneous unexpected ways. Lughnasad begins a series of harvest festivals with a Wickerman or Willow Woman. Mabon (even though we know he isn't a fertility harvest God) oversees our storytelling about balance. The Crone comes in at Samhain to claim her portion of the harvest and to build a bridge to the Ancestors.

Grandmother Spiderwoman teaches us at the full moons, along with many other favorite moon Goddesses when we seek the paths of the Shining Ones. Some people learn to see them.

Because we are both a teaching and healing circle, we also focus on healing in most of our rituals. Some of that work is done through spells. Others parts are accomplished by our guides through meditation in ritual. When someone sends in a need for healing, but are not present, we may make a talisman or poppet and direct healing through it with a cone of power. Or we may include a group Reiki sending for distance healing. A person who is present may be seated in the center for hands-on work. We share messages received from spirit on the spot. This part of a ritual is truly impromptu since we never know who is going to request healing before the ritual, or how that healing should be best approached until the spirits tell us.

How are we structured? The Web PATH Center functions as a church in order to be a tax exempt organization. It is also possible to have not-for-profit corporation status, which we hold on a state level only. Under United States tax law that means as a group we need to meet regularly, have educational programs for adults and children, include family activities, maintain a membership, have a governing body in the local circle, and refrain from political activity as a collective. Since that was always our approach, we find it a comfortable place to be, though we do not use the word *church* in our name or publicity. Too many people think only in terms of Christian connotations if we do.

Regular Meetings

We meet on the 12-13 full moons, the eight sabbats, and for the bi-monthly shamanic circle, which is more than sufficient to meet the legal requirements. Whether there are two people there or 20, we conduct the circle. Consistency is important in this arena. People can count on us.

Education

We offer four levels of Wiccan training; each level involving a minimum of 40 hours' class time; each having its own initiation ceremony. We usually have a weekend shamanic intensive each year in addition to training at our shamanic circles. These two types of training are open to adults and teens over age 12, although Wicca III and IV require youths to wait until at least the age of 18 so they have the maturity to enter into the knowledge. Throughout the year we offer five or six single-day seminars in various healing modalities, psychic skills, or meditation. Some of those are appropriate to children depending on their interests and abilities. Children attend with written parental permission. At our annual SummerFest we offer workshops for adults and children in many of the same areas. We developed a *Frogwarts* curriculum for children under age 10, although later parts of the study need further work.

Family Involvement

Children are welcome at rituals with their parent or guardian. We focus on activities that engage the child in all of us when young people are present. Art, singing, knot magic, shaping magical items with clay, and beading feathers in sacred space with focused intent can help make an esoteric concept real to children and adults. We include time for questions and discussions. Our rituals are visually beautiful. When children are present we may pass a battery-operated candle to cast the circle instead of real flame. We have similar colored lights for the four directions, which they can safely use. Children benefit from learning breath work and grounding right along with adults. These things change our emotions and calm the physical body. We also incorporate storytelling in our rituals, a task which has become easier since Wicca III offers the initiation of the storyteller.

Membership

To continue our emphasis on inclusion, we have a general membership made up from anyone on our mailing list, e-lists and people who attend our circles. These folks are affiliates. We are interested in their opinions and are happy to accept their volunteer service. We have no staff. All of us are volunteers. We also have a voting membership for people age 12 and up which costs $1. Just one. We did not want money to be a barrier to anyone who wished to be at the heart of the Web. We have newly set up supporting membership so that people pledge a specific amount of money per year to chip in on rent, utilities, and seed money for SummerFest.

Governing Body

The Web PATH Center is governed by a council of trustees. Because part of our mission statement is to help define Pagan culture in the 21st Century, we wanted to be watchful of our words. Rather than a board of directors, which seemed to be more authoritarian, we chose a title that evoked a cooperative essence. Although by law the council must organize itself with the traditional officers, they can choose to work by consensus, use rotating chairs to lead meetings and develop new ways to arrange feedback with the membership. We have written by-laws, a bank account, a PayPal account, quarterly meetings and reports, and an annual dinner the Saturday after Samhain. Council members must be voting members. They must be in communication with us regularly (several live far enough away so they could not attend circle or council meetings in person). The internet makes this possible; so do conference calls for council meetings. We have a teen representative on the council to assist us in developing programs for youth and children. They cannot vote on legal matters, but otherwise are fully empowered councilors.

Community

We look good on paper don't we? Does it all work smoothly? No, not all the time. People do not automatically understand intentional community. We lost some ground in the last couple of years because of internal politics. There are too few workers to cover all our bases. We are scrambling to make ends meet, but it is getting better. Lots of people overcommit and then things fall apart exactly when we need them to work. People get mad and go away, or simply wander off with no explanation because their own lives are complicated. Feelings get hurt. Leaders get frustrated. All of us get scared sometimes. What if we set up a great program and nobody comes? These are realities of working with people in groups.

After 20 years on the job, we are still here as The Web. The newsletter is being resurrected as a quarterly effort. Our bank account is getting regular deposits again. We have new members coming on the council as older members leave (there is a maximum number of years to serve before a required hiatus.) The shamanic circle has been restored with new leadership. Rituals continue with experienced ritualists paired with Wicca I students. SummerFest is again a long weekend event. We have increased our local community involvement and have a more public profile.

What can we expect for this year at the Web? The general membership met on New Year's Day (or close to it) to plan out the calendar for the full year. Volunteers will step up to lead ritual. The SummerFest committee will identify itself and we will pick a date. Our rituals will continue. We will offer Wicca I again, and maybe Wicca II.

The newsletter *WebNotes* will continue. We will finish the book 18 of us are writing on *Sacred Sex and Magick* for Moon Books. We will conclude our work on a grounding CD. Perhaps we will start our next project: an oracle deck of cards. We have the artists who can produce it. We also expect to make collages for the four directions. Personally, I would like to see someone become the WebMaster and reinstate our Web Page, which we gave up a few years ago. Some of us mean to make a pilgrimage to Glastonbury for the 2014 Goddess Conference and to visit various sacred sites in the summer. Who knows what else? The possibilities are endless.

The infinite possibilities available to creative spirits makes the Web PATH Center strong as an eclectic practice. We have thought through our choices. We are open to new ideas. We celebrate a new person's background as a different kind of Pagan as long as they come in peace and love. The most important reality is our unity in the Web of consciousness and our universal connections in love which are clearest when we sit in ritual circle together.

Dorothy Abrams is a Central New York feminist Witch, cofounder of the Web PATH Center and author of *Identity and the Quartered Circle*.

The Dianic Tradition and the Core of Witchcraft

Hearth Moon Rising

Then in this dire need she prayed to Diana *to set her free; when lo! she found the prison door unfastened, and easily escaped.* (Charles Godfrey Leland, *Aradia, Gospel of the Witches*[1])

When a new wave of feminism swept the globe in the late 1960s and early 1970s, Dianic Witchcraft emerged as a reclamation of spirituality by, for, and about women. Initiated on Winter Solstice 1971 by friends and followers of Hungarian-American Witch Zsuzsanna "Z" Budapest, Dianic Witchcraft is a spiritual expression of radical feminism, which is differentiated from more moderate forms of feminism by its intention of creating a more feminine world rather than settling for equality within structures created by men.

Obviously creating "a more feminine world" does not mean painting the world with pink nail polish. What exactly does it mean? To answer that question, 70s' feminists began creating their own political caucuses, art collectives, cultural groups, and collective living arrangements, all consisting entirely of women. Even at its inception, members of this movement understood that a definition of feminine by the female, as opposed to male projections of "femininity," would be ongoing, evolving, and multi-generational. The answer to the question, "What is a feminine world?" is one we didn't know then and still don't know today.

But within the Dianic tradition of witchcraft, some features of a feminine spirituality readily emerged. This new form of witchcraft was highly embodied. It focused on women's lived experience as opposed to Platonic idealism. It conceptualized the

Great Goddess as self-generating and self-perpetuating, complete within herself. It emphasized feminine archetypes such as Amazon, Nymph, Hag, Midwife, and Queen, while shifting perception of these archetypes. Above all it sought to affirm women in ways other than their usefulness to men.

Dianic Witchcraft profoundly changed both feminism and religion, including patriarchal religion. 1960s' feminism grew out of a Marxist-socialist perspective that was hostile to the very idea of religion, an attitude that was validated by the subordinate position of women in all the major religions. In 1971 no one was talking about feminism and religion, except to point to the ways religion reinforced patriarchy.[2] While scholarship on matrifocal ancient religions certainly existed, it took a few visionary women to demonstrate that there were spiritual legacies which were not only compatible with feminist goals, but moved them forward.

The Dianic religion in turn inspired more feminist research into pre-Christian religions. Dianic beliefs and practices bled into progressive Christian movements, both Catholic and Protestant, as well as other Pagan traditions. Most of these beliefs did not originate with Dianic priestesses but were nonetheless popularized by them. These included the Maiden-Mother-Crone conception of a woman's lifecycle, the framing of myths such as "Persephone and Demeter" as a woman's life journey, and the ritual celebration of a woman's entrance into full maturity or "Cronehood." Prior to their widespread living practice, the foundational beliefs of Dianic religion were seen as relics of a murky past or isolated indigenous traditions, when they were recognized at all.

While some 19th-century feminists, most notably Matilda Joslyn Gage, Victoria Woodhull and Elizabeth Cady Stanton,[3] tried to convince the world that Christianity needed to change in order to move the cause of women's rights forward, their efforts were largely unsuccessful. It took the living example of an autonomous women's religion to make clear to progressive

Christian sects that women's rights within their organizations meant more than female clergy. The shift in consciousness precipitated by the Dianic movement in turn inspired women in Jewish and American Buddhist traditions to push for a more prominent feminine focus. Today few Christian, Jewish, Buddhist, or even Pagan practitioners would acknowledge a debt to Dianic Witchcraft, but the fact remains that the unprecedented feminine shift in these religions would not have occurred had religion and feminism remained in opposition to one another – and it was Dianic Witchcraft that brought the two together.

Dianic Witchcraft has much in common with Wiccan traditions originating in Britain, though it should not be categorized, as some have described it, as "Gardnerian Wicca without the God." Like other forms of Wicca, we take a gentle view of the world and approach worship with a celebratory mood. We accept the Wiccan Rede and the Threefold Law. Correspondences between directions and elements are the same, and we observe the eight sabbats and the full moon. Like initiates in other Wiccan traditions, we require students to study and work. You do not become a Dianic priestess by saying "I am a witch" three times. That idea originated with a 1960s' political group with the acronym of W.I.T.C.H., which stood for Women's International Terrorist Conspiracy from Hell. This group performed guerilla theater by dressing up as stereotypic witches and going through the motions of "hexing" banks and other corporate entities in front of television cameras. Contrary to popular belief, the Terrorist Conspiracy from Hell was an entirely different outfit.[4]

Like most Wiccan traditions, Dianic witches see the creator as a Goddess who gives birth to a God (among many other things). Although we acknowledge the God as son and lover, he is not the focus of our worship. We view the Goddess as whole and complete. Polarities exist and we do not disparage their use, but in our groups we work with unified energy. The Great Rite is not a part of our liturgy. The emphasis on the Great Goddess has led some to characterize us as a monotheistic religion, but we do recognize and worship many goddesses under many names. Our religion is named specifically for Diana because:

1) Under Roman occupation a large number of Goddesses across Europe were renamed "Diana," so the name Diana epitomizes the concept of the Goddess who is many and one;

2) Diana is described in folklore as the Goddess of the poor and champion of the oppressed; and

3) Diana appears in classical mythology as a Goddess who refuses to marry and prefers the company of women.

Dianic Witchcraft is a women's religion. We initiate only women into our tradition and we usually worship in women-only circles. Another Wiccan tradition calling itself "Dianic," which emerged at roughly the same time as the tradition initiated by Z Budapest, does accept men; but this tradition now calls itself "McFarland Dianic," after its founder Morgan McFarland, to avoid confusion between the two groups.

Not every Dianic coven is started by an initiate of Z Budapest. Some groups are started by women who read Z Budapest's books and the books of other Dianic priestesses. This is considered an acceptable way to begin practicing, and although eventually many of these priestesses seek more formal training, most women in our tradition consider these groups to be Dianic provided they are female-only, serve women through a feminist orientation, and focus on worship of goddesses rather than gods.

When we affirm that Dianics are committed to "serving women and worshiping the Goddess," many people reframe this as "excluding men and not honoring the God." There is a fundamental difference between these two statements. We are moving toward a Goddess-centered world that fully empowers women, rather than rejecting men or gods, and the decisions we make in structuring our tradition and our covens are aimed at furthering this vision. There is also nothing that precludes a Dianic priestess from worshiping a god or circling with a man, no oaths or vows to abjure male contact in spiritual context, although many of our priestesses do choose to work exclusively with feminine divine energy.

An issue of controversy coming from outside our tradition is our policy of limiting participation in ritual to female-born women. Who is and is not appropriate for admission to the circle is up to the discretion of the high priestess, but in most cases trans women are not admitted. It would be hard to imagine a philosophy more incompatible with the embodied experience-based perspective of Dianic worship than the various transgender theories. Whether it's the belief that the transgender individual is "in the wrong body," or the belief that "sex exists only in the mind," or the belief that "identity trumps social-ization," or the belief that being female is a chosen "identity" that can be transient, or the contention that "the phallus is a feminine symbol," or the desire to "celebrate my penis as a female organ," transgender theory cannot be reconciled with the philosophy and mission of the Dianic religion.[5] As far as magic goes, it also does not work well for us to admit trans women to our circles, as admitting a male body to the circle – even a body cosmetically altered by surgery or hormones – changes the magical energy in the group. This is true whether the individual identifies as a man or a woman in their own mind.

It is important to understand that Dianics have no argument with trans women. Their definition of "woman" may be different than ours, but we recognize that they have a right to their own beliefs. Nor do we object to trans women forming their own traditions and borrowing elements of ours. Some Dianic women have generously lent their support and experience to trans women interested in forming their own groups. But at the same time we insist that our boundaries be respected. We insist that our beliefs be tolerated. We insist on the right to define ourselves. It is entirely appropriate, and even necessary, for at least some women to organize socially, politically, and spiritually around our biology. Our biology is, after all, the basis of our oppression under patriarchy.

While many witches look to pre-Christian societies for inspiration on how to structure their practice, Dianics look even further back, to the days before patriarchy. What we call the "matriarchies" of Old Europe and the ancient Mediterranean were sexually egalitarian, relatively peaceful societies with little class stratification, where Goddess worship was widespread.[6] These societies validate our primary focus on the Goddess, since Neolithic Goddess imagery overwhelmingly outnumbers imagery of Gods.[7] Even Ice Age imagery, while predominantly animal rather than human, significantly emphasizes feminine over masculine divine forms.[8] Dianic priestesses are strong consumers of ancient feminine images, often familiar with a wide array of prehistoric art, and thus have been less susceptible than other witches to meretricious attempts to invalidate our core practices and beliefs. We place a high value on pictures to understand our past and document our present.

Feminine imagery also aids in body acceptance, an important value in Dianic spirituality. As females under patriarchy we are evaluated on the appearance of our bodies, while at the same time we are taught to hate our bodies. Worshiping skyclad can aid tremendously in body acceptance, but many women are uncomfortable doing so in mixed-sex gatherings, assuming they will be judged as too fat or too wrinkled or too scarred. Some Dianic covens practice ritual nudity and some do not, but dancing freely in a safe atmosphere, with or without clothing, allows women to fully inhabit their bodies. Paradoxically, by embracing their bodies, women become more adept at consciously moving into out-of-body states.

Along with greater acceptance of body type, Dianic Witchcraft addresses and ceremonially integrates aspects of female biology such as menstruation, childbirth, and menopause. Healing dis/eases of female reproduction, as well as celebration of milestones such as menarche and pregnancy, is often most comfortable and most effective in a well-bonded all-female group. The Maiden-Mother-Crone lifecycle of the Dianic priestess roughly corresponds with reproductive milestones, with the Maiden phase beginning at birth, Mother commencing at delivery of the first child, and Crone emerging at menopause. Where childbirth is delayed or menopause occurs very early, the Mother phase starts at the completion of the first Saturn cycle (roughly age 30) and the Crone phase occurs at the completion of the second Saturn cycle (around age 57). In the Dianic tradition we are all mothers once we reach the Mother phase, our way of acknowledging that women nurture others in a variety of ways.

Witches in most traditions divide their ritual into the categories of "high magic," which involves casting a circle and various invocations, and "low magic" or "kitchen magic," which involves spellcasting that is less ceremonial. While Dianics perform both high and low magic, Dianic priestesses *tend* to include more kitchen magic in their repertoire than other types of witches, of the kind that was historically passed from mother to daughter. This is, however, a generalization and not universally the case. As Z Budapest says, "The Dianic tradition is not something nailed down, etched in stone."[9] There is a great deal of diversity among priestesses and among covens, as Dianics do not like to dictate to other women how to do their magic. Those priestesses trained by Z Budapest also *tend* to be highly creative and spontaneous with their magic. She explains, "We see creativity as a form of prayer; improvisation as a sacred channeling."[10]

Dianics have a reputation for being eclectic, an assessment that doesn't say much about us, considering all the individualistic spiritual expressions that categorize themselves as such. Some valid criticisms have been made regarding the "cafeteria" approach to spiritual practice found in the New Age as a whole. In the worst examples of this approach, group facilitators pull disparate elements of earth-based religions into a framework that looks vaguely Wiccan, and end up with ceremony that bewilders or even offends. Dianic groups are more disciplined, integrating new techniques into a clear foundational base. Still, Dianic rituals can be highly innovative. Ruth Barrett, a Los Angeles-based priestess who has been in the tradition more than 30 years, attributes this innovative tendency to a need to re-create aspects of matrifocal religion that have been forgotten in the thousands of years of patriarchy, explaining, "The Dianic tradition is largely eclectic because we've had to make up everything that was lost."[11]

Along with the creative/innovative tendency of the Dianic tradition itself, many priestesses are initiates of other religious groups, a phenomenon that is not uncommon in witchcraft. Jade River, founder of the Wisconsin-based Re-Formed Congregation of the Goddess – International (RCG-I), believes this comes from the diverse ethnic backgrounds of Dianic priestesses and the desire to integrate ancestral roots into a Dianic framework. She says this is also a motivation for Dianic priestesses seeking advanced formal training.

The RCG-I was started in 1983 as a way to bring various Dianic groups and covens together to define and develop Dianic Witchcraft. Many Dianic covens are quite insular, especially in areas where practicing witchcraft is dangerous. Jade River estimates that a fifth of Dianic priestesses have joined the RCG-I. Since the RCG-I has approximately 3,200 members, this would put the number of practicing Dianics at around 15,000. Growth has mirrored the waxing and waning of the popularity of the feminist movement. The increase in women identifying with feminism, coinciding with better networking through the internet, has meant more interest in recent years, particularly with younger women.

Dianic Witchcraft has an important impact on religious communities that reaches beyond our initiates. Many women in other Pagan sects, and even in the more liberal mainline religious institutions, are aware of our practice and influenced by it. On the whole, however, religion continues to be one of the two main channels where subordination of women is enforced (the other channel being poverty). The existence of a well functioning female-led religion devoted to the interests of females helps women to negotiate greater power within religious structures that include men.

Going forward, the challenge for Dianic Witchcraft will be to maintain our dedication to feminist principles while remaining cognizant of the needs and priorities of contemporary women. The Dianic tradition has maintained integrity through waves of antifeminist backlash coming from the Pagan community as well as the larger society, and it is important that the tradition remain committed to a feminism that is defined by women. Yet while the need for feminism is ongoing, many women do not see a need for a feminist affiliation during times when their lives are going relatively well. During periods when feminism is out of fashion, which have sometimes been quite long, much of women's collective wisdom becomes forgotten. As Jade River puts it, "I would like young women to take what we did and move forward and not reinvent the same thing."[12]

Dianic Witchcraft is a forward-looking tradition. It takes inspiration from humanity's earliest religious beliefs, yet provides a framework that is flexible and allows for innovation. It ties the wisdom of a woman's body, the wisdom of a woman's experience, and the wisdom of a woman's intellect to a Goddess-focused practice. The Goddess Movement is now much larger than the Dianic tradition, yet the tradition's woman-centered autonomy is an integral core of that movement. The Dianic tradition is also a core of witchcraft – that untamed feminine core that eludes the control of reasonable men. The Dianic tradition has produced some of the most powerful witches in the Craft. Supporting Dianic Witchcraft supports the Wiccan, Goddess and feminist communities as a whole and ensures a place for religion in the era of the fully liberated woman.

Hearth Moon Rising lives in the Adirondack Mountains of upstate New York, where she practices a nature-based magical craft. She is an ordained priestess in two traditions (Dianic and Fellowship of Isis) and has taught magic for over twenty years. She is the author of *Invoking Animal Magic: A Guide for the Pagan Priestess.*

Footnotes

1. Charles Godfrey Leland, *Aradia, Gospel of the Witches* (Custer, WA: Phoenix Publishing, 1990), p68.
2. Radical feminist Mary Daly's 1968 *The Church and the Second Sex* (New York: Harper and Row) looks downright modest next to her 1978 *Gyn/Ecology* (Boston: Beacon Press).
3. See *The Garden of Eden; or The Paradise Lost & Found* by Victoria Woodhull (1890) http://www.sacred-texts.com /wmn/tge/index.htm, *Woman, Church and State* by Matilda Joslyn Gage (1893) http://www.sacred-texts.com/wmn/wcs/ and *The Woman's Bible* by Elizabeth Cady Stanton (1895-1898) http://www.sacred-texts.com/wmn/wb/. All accessed September 3, 2013.
4. In the 1980s I knew a former member of the loosely organized W.I.T.C.H., who confirmed that they saw themselves as a socialist-feminist political group. Robin Morgan in *Going Too Far: The Personal Chronicle of a Feminist* (New York: Random House, 1978) also states that the group knew nothing about Witchcraft, although they apparently understood that it had something to do with women's

empowerment. Some former members of W.I.T.C.H. may have later become Dianics.

5. Most people are aware of the "trapped in the wrong body" narrative, but this idea is growing out of favor with prominent trans theorists, as scientific evidence for a significantly differentiated female brain continues to be lacking. Julia Serano, author of the classic *Whipping Girl: A Transsexual Woman on Sexism and the Scapegoating of Femininity* (Berkeley, CA: Seal Press, 2007) characterizes this narrative as "Those confessional tell-alls that non-trans people seem to constantly want to hear from transsexuals…" p1. Serano advances a more current theory in an April 2012 article in *Ms. Magazine,* "Trans Feminism: There's No Conundrum About It." http://msmagazine.com/blog/2012/04/18/trans-feminism-theres-no-conundrum-about-it/. Joelle Ruby Ryan, a lecturer in Women's Studies at the University of New Hampshire, has been a leader in the international movement to prevent feminist meetings from occurring without trans inclusion. This individual narrated an autobiographical video on February 4, 2013 called "Transilience" on trans perspective. http://www.youtube.com/watch?v=gZ7eeRCdX9k. Riki Wilchins, founder of the organization, The Transsexual Menace, and regular contributor to the longstanding LGBT newspaper, *The Advocate,* has argued that acceptance from others of personal gender identity is a basic right, as in this December 18, 2012 piece, "Op-Ed: 'But You Can't Really Be Her Mom.'" http://www.advocate.com/commentary/riki-wilchins/2012/12/18/you-can%E2%80%99t-really-be-her-mom. Toni D'orsay, a blogger at *Dyssonance,* explains the sometime feminine nature of the phallus in the article "Revisiting the Fear Phallic" at http://www.dyssonance.com/revisiting-the-fear-phallic/. As D'orsay explains in this March 30, 2012 article, "…the statement that indicates that the penis is not a female

organ is relying on a mode of thinking and a world of thought that is, in and of itself, an oppressive act."

6. See Riane Eisler, *The Chalice and the Blade* (San Francisco: Harper and Row, 1988). In the last 20 years, archeologists and historians have scrutinized Neolithic Europe and the Middle East for indicators of violence and for alternative theories to refute the existence of cultures that revered the divine feminine. When such evidence or alternate explanation has been found, however sketchy, it has been hailed as definitive takedown of the Goddess Movement, rather than a sign that matriarchal theories need to be rethought, refined, and understood in less absolute terms. Max Dashu responded to the bias and not-so-hidden agenda in this new scholarship in her 2000 article "Knocking Down Straw Dolls: A Critique of Cynthia Eller's *The Myth of Matriarchal Prehistory*." http://www.suppressedhistories.net/articles/eller.html.

7. Marija Gimbutas, *The Language of the Goddess*. (San Francisco: Harper and Row, 1989), p. 175.

8. Paul G. Bahn and Jean Vertut, *Journey Through the Ice Age*, (London, Seven Dials, 1998), p160.

9. Zsuzsanna Budapest, email message to HMR, May 23, 2013.

10. Ibid.

11. Ruth Barrett, in discussion with HMR, June 9, 2013.

12. Jade River, in discussion with HMR, June 2, 2013.

Traditional British Old Craft

Melusine Draco

Regardless of where we live in the world, traditional British Old Craft is influenced by our immediate surroundings and the contours of the local landscape. This means stepping outside our protective bubble and interacting with Nature as a *participant*, not merely an observer who sees their natural surroundings as "beautiful and welcoming". To understand Nature is to live as a part of Nature, and ultimately to become one with its changing patterns and cycles, to synchronise one's own personal psychic or magical energy with natural tidal forces and the elements.

We may sit meditating by a rippling stream, watching the sunlight dance in the water as it trips over the stones and pebbles in its path – but do we allow our minds to explore the greater picture of where that crystal clear water comes from? Do we realise that this stream began its brief chapter of life being drawn up as vapour from the ocean and falling as rain on the hills and mountain sides, before flowing down into the river valley, bringing rocks and stones tumbling in its wake? Do our magical energies focus on the stream; the rainfall on the mountain; or the ocean? Are we constantly aware of the force of that water-flow throughout the seasons – the spring floods; the summer drought; the clogging of the channel with autumn leaves and the frozen surface in winter. Or does our concept of Elemental Water begin and end with the symbolic bowl of tap water marking the Eastern quarter in our magic Circle?

Let us also consider what we blithely refer to as 'Earth Mysteries' that often produce a mild tingling sensation, which sets the pendulum swinging; or a burst of warm energy in our hands and feet. But do we stop to think that this could be caused by the swirling molten layer under the Earth's crust, creating the electro-magnetic field that surrounds the planet by the spinning outer crust around the solid part of the inner core? Or is our Elemental Earth just a quiet ramble in the countryside and a container of sand marking the Northern quarter?

An old-time witch, would not, of course, have known about these scientific discoveries – or rather they would have known about the *effect*, if not the cause – having learned why and how to harness these most magical of natural energies, and in which location to find them. These natural phenomena may have been viewed as messages from the "gods", but the energy manifested in their wake would have been utilised by the wisemen and women in the community for practical magic in all its forty shades of grey. They would have known that the natural energy from the fields and hedgerows would lack the darker, primordial elements of the woodlands and forest – and tailored their spell-craft accordingly. The seashore with is direct link to the deep ocean would require a totally different approach than an urban landscape where natural energies were concealed and often smothered behind a thick veil of "stupidity, greed and bustle".

Even more importantly, we now know that some geological formations are better suited for magical or creative working than others, an idea that was mooted by Dion Fortune in her novel, *The Goat-Foot God:*

> Now the best place to get the kind of experiences you want is on chalk. If you think of it, all the earliest civilisation in these islands was on the chalk … Avebury's on the chalk; and St Albans is on the chalk …

While Christopher Tilley in *A Phenomenology of Landscape*, gives a wider overview of the topographic features of the prehistoric landscape that attracted our distant ancestors' attention: an affinity with the coast; mountain escarpments and spurs; the ridges, valleys and chalk downlands. Obviously, the most important aspect of each site being not what is seen above ground, but **the geological formation beneath our feet.**

There are, of course, many different types of rock that make up the Earth's surface and each of them will have certain positive or negative magical/creative properties. As an example, the following were found to be the best and the worst when it comes to drawing from, or stifling, magical/creative energy.

The Best: Slate

Slate is a widespread, metamorphic rock commonly found inter-layered with sedimentary strata and with rocks of volcanic origin. Once we understand that *quartz* is very abundant in slate and may form as much as 70% by weight of the rock, it is not difficult to see why this particular material generates so much Earth energy – quartz being one of the most powerful crystals on the planet. Magical, psychic and creative working on slate packs a very distinctive punch, especially if the slate layers are close to the surface.

The Worst: Clay

Clay – the name derives from Old English *clæg* meaning "sticky" – is a widespread sedimentary rock with grains too small to be seen under any but the most powerful microscope, and may form in many different geological environments throughout the world. The most extensive layers are found in both deep and shallow marine deposits, in moraines (piles of debris) left behind by receding glaciers, and in zones of pre-existent rocks (especially granite) that have been altered by hydrothermal fluids. Try walking through heavy clay and it immediately becomes apparent why Earth energy is often "blocked" or sluggish. Magical working on clay involves a lot of energy-generating techniques by the practitioner, and unless there is a considerable amount of experience (and knowledge) to draw on, things may take a long time to come to fruition.

Where I live in the Glen of Aherlow, in Southern Ireland, for example, beneath the lush greenery the mountains are Old Red Sandstone – a tough enduring rock formed during the Caledonian Foldings, the mountain-building period of the Earth's long history. The pressure caused the underlying softer Silurian rocks to fold into great ridges; and over millions of years the erosion dust compacted to form this magnificent range of red sandstone mountains. The Galtees are Ireland's highest inland mountain range, a high ridge which rises up almost sheer from the surrounding plain. Two major Ice Age periods have affected the area, and the rounded summits of the Galtees are due to the higher parts being above the ice. This freeze-thaw action on the higher peaks gradually wore them away to form the stony, scree-covered summits we see today. This glacial action also formed cirques (or corries) on the higher slopes – rocky amphitheatres, which are now five gloomy lakes.

And as I have observed in *Magic Crystals, Sacred Stones* and *The Hollow Tree: A Beginner's Guide to the Tarot and Qabalah*, because sandstone is highly susceptible to weathering and decomposition, and ultimately crumbling to dust, we can safely assign it to the **Element of Earth**. Or more precisely, the "**Earthy part of Earth**" symbolised by the Princess of Disks in the Tarot, who represents the "element of the brink of Transfiguration". **She has been depicted with her sceptre descending into the Earth where the point becomes a diamond, and her shield denoting the "twin spiral forces of Creation in perfect equilibrium".**

This might go a long way in explaining why in the five years we have lived in the Glen, I've managed to complete ten books in quick succession, several of which had been lying dormant for several years. The energies of the Glen are "dark" – not in any negative sense – but because the primitive history of the place is unchanged and unchanging. And if, like me, you are someone who is attuned to primitive energies, then the magical/creative urges will be stimulated with a vengeance when living in such a magnificent location. The mountains are never the same on consecutive days: the summits are either capped with snow, radiating in the mellow tones of sunset, shimmering in a soft blue haze, cloaked by low-lying clouds and soft rain, or (on rare occasions) crystal clear images of a hot summer day when sheep are seen as tiny pin-pricks of white against the green. And when the river is in high-flood, the Glen turns into a vast lake, just as it was before people came to inhabit this part of Ireland.

The area also has a wealth of prehistoric monuments, the earliest of which is a passage-tomb at Shrough, on the Slievenamuck Ridge (immediately behind our cottage), and south of Tipperary Town, which dates to Neolithic times (c.4000–2400BC); with many prehistoric monuments, such as standing stones, surviving in upland areas on the slopes of the Knockmealdown and the Galtee mountain ranges. In the western part of the county, around Emly (where we lived before moving to the Glen) and Lattin, there is a dense concentration of barrows, earth-built burial monuments from the Bronze and Iron Ages (c.2400BC-AD400). In legendary terms, Darby's Bed, like most Irish passage tombs, is located on a hilltop site, near Galbally on Duntryleague Hill – the westerly end of Slievenamuck Ridge. This great megalith is said to be the grave of Olill Olum, one of the early Kings of Munster. The name Duntryleague is derived from Dún-Trí-Liag, meaning the "fort of three pillar stones", and Diarmuid and Gráinne are also said to have rested there in their flight from the angry Fionn MacCumhaill. A path through the forest leads to this amazing burial ground where one enormous rock slab rests across a number of upright stones. So the ancient people of Ireland were most definitely drawn to this place because of the atmosphere and it still retains much of its magic.

But before you respond that this "creative stimulus" is merely wishful thinking on the part of the writer, I would have to add that I experienced similar literary outpourings when living in my homeland of Wales, near the Preseli Mountains. These hills are also dotted with prehistoric remains, including evidence of Neolithic settlement, and in 1923 the bluestone from the hills was identified with that used to build the inner circle of Stonehenge. Archaeologists have since pinpointed the precise place from where the bluestones were removed in about 2500BC – a small crag-edged enclosure at one of the highest points of the 1,008ft high Carn Menyn mountain. The stones were then moved 240 miles to the famous site at Salisbury Plain. This discovery came a year after scientists proved that the remains of a "band of brothers" found near Stonehenge were Welshmen who transported the stones. The skeletons were found by workmen laying a pipe on Boscombe Down and chemical analysis of their teeth revealed they were brought up in South West Wales. Experts believed the family accompanied the stones on their epic journey from the Preseli Hills to Salisbury Plain.

By contrast, the time between living in Wales and Ireland was spent in the flat, reclaimed land of Suffolk and rural Leicestershire, and produced hardly anything at all of a creative or magical nature. To get any form of reaction it was necessary to take the dog for a long walk to a spot that proved itself to be particularly strong on magical/creative energies, and that was the granite outcrop at Markfield (Charwood Forest in Leicestershire) that rises up from the Midlands *clay* plain. These rocks are more closely comparable with those of many parts of Wales and represent some of the oldest known anywhere in England. On the western side of this central plain, the magical Malvern Hills are also unlike any other outcrop in England and Wales, and may represent a slice of pre-Cambrian base-rock, which is only found at the surface in north-west Scotland! Call it co-incidence if you like, but weekends spent in the Malverns also produced a surge of creative energy that quickly diminished after returning home to the plain. The Suffolk sojourn produced absolutely nothing at all, to the point of atrophy – whereas a friend who is a professional photographer draws endless inspiration (both creative and magical) from the misty fens and salt marshes.

- Once you have located what appears be a suitable site, try to pinpoint your own personal energy spot by using a pendulum that contains an element of quartz. Dowse the site thoroughly and calculate where the energy is the strongest from the pendulum's reaction.
- If a location seems unsuitable for magical or inspirational working, then a short journey might make all the difference. For example: the short distance between the clay plain levels at Charnwood and the granite outcrop was only a daily dog's walk away from each other.
- If your energy point is a woodland glade, or the corner of a double hedge, see how well this works with the pendulum and mark the spot for future working.
- An important point to remember is that these energy spots have a habit of moving around and it is necessary to check from time to time that you are still "plugged in" to your source.

As traditional witchcraft became the province of the more educated, the raising of these natural energies by automatically "plugging-in" to the location was supplanted by the use of ceremony and ritual to enhance and consolidate group working. The state of "just being", i.e. natural ability, was sidelined as the different splinter groups created histories and traditions for themselves. For example, the Gardnerians elevated the Goddess over the God; the Alexandrians introduced an element of Egyptian influence; while the Clan of Tubal Cain developed along other lines – all with basic undertones of Freemasonry in their rites.

It must be said that adopting these separate identities for an individual group or Path does not invalidate the claims of traditional witchcraft. The symbolism chosen to represent any particular group was to provide a coherent whole on which the group could focus during its magical working. The original reason behind the choice of focus would often have its local significance for the founding members of the group, but be lost in the intervening years for today's participants. Added to this, contemporary uses and meanings often differ between locations, and the original significance would become obscured or corrupted with each new generation of witches – especially once the founders have passed on to become the Ancestors.

The language of traditional Craft has always been "hidden" and, more often than not, based on instinct and intuition, rather than book learning and rote. In fact, Craft learning is about 40% information and 60% intuition, but it's also about realising when intuition is telling us that we don't have all the information and that we need to go out to seek it. More often than not, those answers we will be found in Nature, rather than by trawling through books, or in the words of wisdom from the latest Pagan guru. The watch-word for any traditional witch should always be "Why?" followed closely by "How?".

Neither should we overlook the power or psychic energy that can be raised at old sacred sites, but one thing that should always be borne in mind is that "ancient" is not always sacred.

And even those popular tourist sites that were sacred are now so defiled by the tramping feet of the thousands of idly curious that they will possibly need generations to recharge the batteries. If we take another hint from the writings of Dion Fortune, however, we can find what we are looking for if we locate the "lines of force" *between* the remains of ancient worship by drawing a line from one to another on the map. "You will get quite enough power without being overwhelmed by it," she wrote.

As far as our home-grown beliefs are concerned, all we can know with any certainty is that prior to the arrival of the Celts, the indigenous beliefs of the people were focussed on Ancestor-worship and an afterlife, with the main points of the yearly cycle being observed at the solstices as indicated by the alignment of the numerous ancient monuments that litter the landscape. A more localised core of devotion was the attraction of "watery places" such as springs and the water margin of lakes, fens and rivers: very similar, in fact, to ancient Shinto beliefs, which are still observed in Japan today.

Christopher Tilley also expounds his belief that the prehistoric landscape reflected the beliefs, myths, legends and stories of the period: for instance, when sunset at the summer solstice coincides with a chink in the hills on the skyline. At other times it may be more local or intimate, such as when an ancestral burial mound is, or is not, visible behind something as insignificant as a low hillock, or indeed another barrow. "Either way, the play, the player and the landscape that once lived in all of their minds, are inseparable." The traditional witch must be mindful of all these things, whether channelling the energy for spell casting in a mountain cave, woodland glade or an urban sitting room.

Neither should we think that because *we* refer to ourselves as "Pagan" or "witch" that this gives us immediate access to the power generated at any of these locations. It is not ours by right, and permission *must* be sought and given before proceeding. When interacting with Nature we may find that the way is closed to us by an unseen but impenetrable barrier, as if the *genius loci* is telling us that we are not welcome. Our surrounding landscape *does* influence the way magical and creative workings come to fruition, and also dictates the amount of effort needed to be put into the ritual or creative project to bring about the desired effect. Understanding what lies beneath our feet will enhance our magical and creative ability, especially if we can learn to plug-in to the natural energy of the place.

These were the lessons taught by Bob and Meriem Clay-Egerton in the Coven of the Scales. That it wasn't necessary to rely on ritual, Circle casting, chanting and dancing to generate magical energy, it is there, all around us on a permanent basis. It means that a natural witch can be on her contacts in seconds; knowing what type of energy is needed to cure a headache, or channel the strength to walk the death-path with confidence after being diagnosed with a terminal illness. **It really is a belief that can move mountains – if the application is right.** These seemingly insurmountable obstacles do not necessarily mean that the doors to Old Craft are permanently barred; the road may be long and arduous, but the true seeker will get there in the end – and will not regret the struggles and hardship.

Mélusine Draco originally trained in the magical arts of traditional British Old Craft with Bob and Mériém Clay-Egerton. She has been a magical and spiritual instructor for over 20 years with Arcanum and the Temple of Khem, and writer of numerous popular books including *The Traditional Witchcraft* series and *The Dictionary of Magic & Mystery*. She lives in Ireland near the Galtee Mountains.

Hedge Witchcraft

Harmonia Saille

Hedge witchcraft is shamanic in nature. The solitary hedge witch rides the hedge, the boundary between this world and the next, crossing between civilization and the wilds of the otherworld.

Many people believe that hedge witchcraft is a nature, kitchen or green pathway, or even that it is another name for a solitary witch. In part this comes from the idea of the witch of old who lived in the cottage on the margins of society, the hedge separating her from the rest of the village. However, every hedge witch is individual, and her or his practices may differ. In fact a hedge witch may, as part of their craft workings, practice one or all of the above, or a host of other things, such as healing or magic. What really defines the hedge witch – one thing they will all have in common – is hedge riding.

You will find that witches and Pagans who follow other pathways may also hedge ride, although they may call it shamanic journeying or something similar. This, however, may not be the main feature of their practice.

For the hedge witch, being individual means they will build on the different aspects of their practice alongside developing their hedge riding skills. Therefore, to discuss here an exact pathway is impossible. Hedge witchcraft is always subjective. It is individual to each witch. Here, although I will talk about hedge riding as this is the one thing hedge witches have in common, I will also discuss divination and healing as they often come with the purpose of hedge riding, and the deep connection with nature in our own world or the otherworld.

First, where did the term hedge witch originate? Eric de Vries discusses the meaning in his book *Hedge-Rider* (2008) saying that Dutch word *Heks* (which is Dutch for "witch"), comes from the

Middle Dutch word *Haghetesse,* meaning "spirit on the hedge" and that the German word *hexe* come from middle German *hagazusse* meaning "soul on the fence". In Old Norse it is *Hagzissa* and Old English *Haegtesse* (today we know this as "hag").

If we look to the *The Havamal,* the verses below (two different translations of verse 156) concern those that shapeshift (the witch) and who fly at night.

Verses 147–165 of *The Havamal* are charms. Depending on which translation you follow, reciting the charm can cause either the hedge rider to show their true self and return home, or the rider's spirit to become separated from their physical body. *The Havamal* is from the *Poetic Edda* of the 13th Century but perhaps composed earlier.

I know this the tenth:
If I see the hedge-riders magically flying high,
I can make it so they go astray
Of their own skins, and of their own souls.
(Nigel Pennick, *Havamal, Complete Illustrated Guide to Runes,* 2002)

A tenth I know, what time I see
House-riders flying on high;
So can I work, that wildly they go,
Showing their true shapes,
Hence to their own homes.
(Henry Adams Bellows, *Hovamol,* verse 156, *The Poetic Edda,* 1936)

The hedge rider of ancient times then flew to the otherworld to consult with spirits and gods for the purposes of magic or prophecy, often shape shifting. The hedge rider of modern times will do this too. Shape shifting is also something the experienced hedge rider will engage in.

Before moving on to the principals of hedge riding I will first briefly discuss the importance of nature in hedge witchcraft, followed by divining and healing as a common part of the hedge witch's practice.

The Importance of Nature in Hedge Witchcraft

When the hedge rider crosses the hedge between worlds, she or he moves from civilization to the wild otherworld. When crossing the hedge we work with spirits of nature and the ancestral spirits. As Pagans we are more often animists and believe in the relatedness of all things. We work with plants, rocks, and animal guides, and with water, trees, fire and wind. In fact try to do our best to live in universal harmony. Therefore, nature is important to hedge witchcraft in general.

Being a hedge witch does not just mean sitting at home riding the hedge and nothing else, but engaging in strengthening skills and senses, and in connecting spiritually. A sense of the spirit of place is paramount to spirituality, and one of the best ways to connect with spirit is outdoors. The hedge witch will find a natural sacred space within the forest, on the hill or close to the lake.

When we are in the countryside or park we often feel the wild otherness of the spirit there, and that we are privileged to be there – in magical territory. When we walk in the fields or paddle in the stream we adapt ourselves to our surroundings, and become a part of nature. We use all our senses: we breathe in the fresh smell of rain on grass; hear the wind rustling the leaves of the birch; feel the coldness of the water; we might call out to hear the echo; and we sense the spirit in all things. We sense the spirit of place, the spirit in the mountain, the spirit in the stream, the spirit in the tree or rock.

In Ireland there is a strong sense of spirit in the landscape, the wells, portals, stone circles, raths, lakes, rivers, sea, forest and many other places, and it is easy to understand the need to connect with them if you live or visit there. In the same way, you cannot help but connect with the local gods and goddesses in the areas around where you live, even if you follow another pantheon. Visiting magical and spiritual areas can help you connect with the spirits that reside there. Alternatively, you may find a place where you find it easier to connect with your own ancestral spirits. Connecting with the "Spirit of Place" is an essential part of hedge witchcraft.

When you view the valley, forest, river, and hills around your home be aware of your relationship with creation and that you are part of that creation, a single continuity – and therefore have your place in the universe. All is sacred and one.

The nature connection is important to hedge riding and the ability to connect with what you experience in the other realms. To connect with and understand what you see, whom you meet, and what you learn.

Divination and Healing

Divination may not seem to have much to do with hedge riding, yet it does. One of the purposes of hedge riding is to seek answers to questions for others or ourselves. This includes conversing with animal and spirit guides, and often the use of crystals. Scrying, using crystals or water, is something that is common in shamanic journeying and so it is in hedge riding. Often runes or symbols may appear which will need interpreting in conjunction with what is around you, and what you may have seen or experienced. Therefore, learning to read symbols and honing your divining skills are essential if you travel to the other realms.

The hedge witch will divine using various methods as part of his or her practice, sometimes using it in combination with hedge or folk magic through hedge riding. Hedge riding may be part of the spell a hedge witch puts together. The hedge witch will hedge ride to discover what the nature of a problem is, and then afterwards incorporate this knowledge into the spellwork.

Divination may also be used to discover the nature of a health problem. A hedge witch who specializes in healing, or perhaps uses it occasionally, will travel to the other realms to help heal themselves or to seek help for others. This may include speaking to their own animal guide and asking it to converse with the animal guide of the inflicted person. The hedge witch will seek advice from spirit guides or bathe in the healing pools and rivers of the otherworld realms.

Hedge Riding
The hedge witch will cross the hedge to seek help from the spirits and elementals that reside there for healing, strength, spiritual enlightenment, protection, sometimes simply to look for messages or solutions to problems, and for help in spell work, and knowledge, but mostly to gain wisdom. For what is knowledge without wisdom? A hedge witch will never cross the hedge for magical empowerment or for material gain.

Hedge riding is an individual experience and riders work with their own animal and spirit guides.

Hedge riding should never be undertaken lightly. It is important to gain initial shamanic training if you can. As a rider, you also need to be very aware of the dangers of the otherworld and to protect yourself before journeying, and ground yourself after journeying. Most of all do not attempt journeying if you have ever suffered or are prone to suffer mental illness such as psychosis. This is very important.

Shape shifting should also not be attempted except by the experienced hedge rider.

Altered State of Consciousness
To journey to the other realms you need to achieve an ASC (altered state of consciousness). This is a state that is accomplished by both natural and induced means, through which visionary messages are received and mystical experiences occur.

In an ASC, your mind works differently than when you are fully awake in this everyday reality. Your mind and spirit are in essence separate from your body. With ASC, you are working just below the surface of full consciousness. This is opposed to the "unconscious" in which things are hidden from you. In an ASC, we are always consciously aware of what we are doing.

Steering away from drugs, there are much safer ways to achieve an ASC. Great concentration is required and perhaps the most popular is drumming, music for shamans, rattling, dancing, chanting, or listening to your own heartbeat or, of course, a combination of methods.

When you are in the otherworld, you know the difference from ordinary reality. You cannot control the scenery or what you see or whom you meet.

In an ASC, we are lucid and able to control our movements. To achieve an ASC it helps if you see yourself as an integral part of the universe. Everything is connected above and below, the planets, earth and everything on earth – everything seen and unseen.

The Three Worlds or Realms

The otherworld has three realms, which in themselves have levels. The lower realm for instance has an even lower level, the underworld. Access to the three worlds is often through a tree. The roots are the portal to the lower world, the trunk the middle world and the branches the upper world. Sometimes a cave provides the portal to the other realms. Whatever method you use, generally there is a tunnel. By the time the experienced hedge rider emerges from the other side of this tunnel they will be in the lower realm. If they wish to travel onwards to the upper worlds this is often done by climbing the tree and/or travelling onwards by boat or air.

The **lower** realm is an earthy place of natural landscape and primal beauty. This realm has almost any type of terrain and scenery and you will find forests, rivers, oceans, mountains, hills, valleys, dales, ice and snow, desert and jungle. Seasonal, it can be spring, winter, summer or autumn.

Animals, fish, birds and insects inhabit this world, and you will find squirrels, rabbits, hares, lions, tigers, snakes, lizards, dolphins, salmon, eagles, butterflies, dragonflies, bees, bears, wolves, deer and mice.

The hedge rider will meet people here too; spirit guides sometimes visit though they dwell mainly in the upper world. They might also meet animal guides, the ancestors, and nature spirits.

The lower realm is often the easiest realm to access. This realm is where the rider often first meets their animal guides. Riders visit this realm to look for guiding messages or simple answers to queries of their own or those of others.

There is another realm that you can access through the lower realm, though there are other ways, this is the underworld and a place of lost souls, which may be best to avoid if you are inexperienced. Shamanic practitioners access this world during psychopomp work.

The **middle** realm is closely associated with our own. The veil is thin and you may often travel in and out. Here riders choose to travel forward or backward in time. When journeying there, you can end up anywhere, a house, city, country or in the countryside. Just as our own world is filled with dangers, this world can be too. Creatures and people you meet here can be tricky and you will find evil as well as good, so take care. In hedge riding, it is best to avoid this realm if you are inexperienced unless you are travelling into your past (to visit the past you or perhaps your ancestors), or into your future (to meet the future you). Have this intent fully in your mind before riding there.

The **upper** realm is a place of great beauty: tropical islands, landscapes of cloud and mists, of jungles and waterfalls, mountains and valleys. This is where the spirits that exist on a higher vibration dwell. Here you will often meet your spirit guides young and old, the wise ones, the gods and goddesses. These guides can come in all guises, angelic, goddesses, wise men and women, the old crone and Native American. Animals, fish, birds and insects also reside there and your animal guides will follow you there. Among the creatures you may meet in the upper world are eagles, deer, salmon, butterflies, herons, bees and snakes.

In the landscape you may see magnificent waterfalls, caves, mountains, bridges, ravines, white beaches, lakes and pools.

Riders visit this realm for healing purposes, to gain wisdom and for knowledge. Scrying is something you may do in this realm in dark pools of water, or you may use other forms of divination to seek answers. The symbolism is powerful here, so it is important, once you come out of your ASC, immediately to write down experiences making note of anything significant. You can then make sense of these by viewing everything you have learnt and seen as a whole. This is where interpretation skills are necessary.

Animal Guides

Animal guides play an important part in hedge riding. The animal guide can be a bird, a fish or a mammal, but generally it is a wild creature not a domesticated one.

With otherworld animal guides you do not choose them but, rather, they have always been with you and they appear in the realms having previously been "unseen" by you (except perhaps occasionally in dreams). So, although you might imagine that a wolf, bear, eagle or stag is your animal guide, you may well find it is a hare, turtle, or even an elephant.

Your animal companion can run, walk, swim, or fly beside you. The guide is company for you so you do not feel alone. It will give you strength, confidence, and added protection. You might be able to communicate with it in some way, but more often than not telepathically. You will also feel a deep connection with it, almost as if you are one being.

It seems then that everyone has animal guides throughout their lives, but perhaps never gets to meet them, as they will never travel the realms.

To meet your guide, you need to be patient and open to meeting it. Using a shaman rattle before riding can encourage your animal guide to come to you. You will have no problem recognizing it as you will find that it will appear several times in successive journeys, or accompany you throughout a journey.

Spirit Guides

Spirit aides come in all shapes and forms and are an added form of protection and guidance in the otherworld. You can have more than one spirit guide.

It can take time to meet your spirit guides and they can appear in many guises. They appear several times, or in a significant way, that shows you they are there for you, to guide, protect and advise you. People wonder why their guides are often Native Americans or druids, and it is a bit of a cliché, but guides often take a form that is most comfortable for us.

Spirit guides may pass you a message, this can be directly with speech, a silent message through gestures; the guide may show you something such as paper or symbol, or pass on the message telepathically.

Remember to always thank your guides.

People and Creatures of the Otherworld

You may not meet many people or creatures in the otherworld until you have completed many ridings. As you become familiar with the worlds, people begin to appear. You may see almost anyone, goddesses and gods, or archetypal figures such as the hero, prince, princess, queen or king, witch or crone, wise men and women, the mother figure, villagers, grandfather or even a child. Creatures are most often wild animals.

What you see has nothing to do with your everyday practice. So if you follow a Norse pantheon you will not necessarily see Norse gods and goddesses or spirit guides, or Celtic or Greek. If you do then you will need to question if you are conjuring them up, and are pathworking not journeying, as in journeying you have no control on what you see or in what form it appears.

Protection

It is advisable to protect yourself during otherworld travel, as there are both positive and negative entities on the other side of the hedge. We never know what we might meet there.

One of the simplest methods of protection is the blue or golden pool of light generated from the solar plexus area and surrounding us like a forcefield in an oval or egg shape. We form this pool of light around us by visualizing it emanating from the solar plexus area just below the breastbone. As it spreads through and around us covering us completely, we deepen the colour to strengthen it. Being aware of it keeps it in place. It will dissipate naturally in time if we do not mentally keep it there.

In addition, you can hold an amulet of protection or wear one.

Your accompanying power animal or spirit guide will help protect you. If you have not met your animal guide/s then your first journeys should be to achieve this.

Lastly, the power of your own mind to reject evil is important.

The Hedge Witch Path

The hedge witch's practice, as you see from above, will certainly include riding the hedge. Divining, hedge (folk) magic, and often healing, will also feature as these are also elements of hedge riding. The rest of the hedge witch's practice is individual. The hedge witch's pathway is not just that of a solitary witch but a dedicated and meaningful one. It is not a pathway of the easy option, but one of years of hard work, always learning, experiencing, helping, healing, and sharing.

The hedge witch will have his or her own ethic and will build his or her own way of working. But I think most hedge witches would agree that hedge witchcraft is a way of life.

Harmonia Saille is an author and hedge witch who holds workshops on spirituality, divination and other subjects both locally and at international spiritual events. She is the author of *Pagan Portals: Hedge Witchcraft* and *Pagan Portals: Hedge Riding* and lives in Ireland.

Solitary Witchcraft

Highland Hedgewitch

When asked to contribute to a book celebrating the 60th anniversary of Gerald Gardner's book, *Witchcraft Today* I was little taken aback. I am a relative newcomer to the Pagan world after being an Anglo Catholic for many years. I hadn't read the book, and was unsure how relevant it would be in the 21st Century. However, from the start I was captivated by Gerald's simple timeless prose and felt taken into his confidence from page one. It was a wonderful simplistic view of witchcraft from his era and the distant past. How lovely to have this snapshot in time, this verbal adventure back into the early days of witchcraft. As I progressed further I couldn't help but wonder how he would have felt could he have been witness to the internet revolution and how it has changed the face of witchcraft and Paganism for many all over the world.

When Gerald wrote the book, the laws prohibiting any practise of witchcraft had only just been repealed, some three years earlier. Witches still celebrated sabbats and practised in private. The law may have changed, but small-minded Britain hadn't progressed that far. People were still worried what their neighbours would say. Covens were still mainly family and a selectively chosen few, for fear of discovery. Although the witch trials were over, gossip and taunts were not. There was still a view held by some, encouraged by the Church, that you were in league with the devil if you were Pagan, Heathen, or a witch. Those who followed the crooked path were into the dark arts, and were best avoided for fear of bewitching or worse.

Witches had been portrayed as evil, against God and villainised for centuries. Yet there had been a time in the distant past when they were the person you went to for help, for cures to common ailments and fertility charms. It wasn't just wives and mothers who consulted the wise woman of the village. Those who worked the land would seek her counsel on the weather. She would have followed the wheel of the year and had knowledge of the seasons, it made sense to ask her advice. However, she was also blamed should cattle become sick, or someone die. She walked a thin line in village life. No wonder, again, that in time she would hide her knowledge and her true path.

As I ventured deeper in the history of witchcraft I found myself emotionally exhausted by the stories of torture. Gerald doesn't hold back with his graphic descriptions of horrific pain and degradation that the interrogators felt impelled to carry out on the victims. No wonder they would confess to anything; you would agree with any preposterous story to put an end to your suffering. Even if that meant your false confession would result in your own death. One such episode is recorded from Aldous Huxley's book *The Devils of Loudun*. It tells of the torture and death of someone called Grandier, accused of bewitching a group of nuns in 1634.

"In the presence of two apothecaries and several doctors Grandier was stripped, shaved all over and then systematically pricked to the bone with a long, sharp probe..." It goes on to say, "through the bricked up windows, the prisoner's screams could be heard."

Gerald sought to inform the masses about modern-day witch-craft. Far from being a dead religion, it was starting to find its place not only in the UK, but also over continents. Gerald was initiated into a local coven, and allowed to tell some of its secrets, though some topics were obviously not up for discussion. During his time within the coven he attended rituals and sabbats at his home and within the woods nearby. It appears that some, if not the majority of these, were enjoyed sky-clad and not thought to be a perversion or with the intention of an orgy, but because the coven found it easier and more natural to work their magic this way. Today, albeit the 21ˢᵗ Century, people's prudish attitudes to nakedness have changed little. It would still be frowned upon, and of course against the law, for a group of people to gather in a public place without clothing in order to work magic or in fact to do anything!

There are few references to solitary witches. It seems that during Gerald's time it was mainly covens who practised. I got the impression that the self-initiated were not viewed as serious about their craft. The only "true" witch was one who had inherited her gift or knowledge or was initiated into the coven by the Priestess. Solitary witches appeared to be second class citizens.

Literature has done little to enhance the image of witches, whether in covens or solitary practitioners. I wonder who was responsible for the image of the witch we have today, black pointed hat, hooked crooked nose, usually old, unattractive, flying on a broomstick probably with her cauldron and a cat in tow. When I was growing up in the 1970s I was brought up with very negative stereotypical, images of witches.

We're witches of Halloween oooohhhh
Our faces are ugly and green oooohhhh
We fly around at night
And give you such a fright
We're witches of Halloween oooohhhh
We hang about with bats
And wear strange pointy hats
We're witches of Halloween oooohhhh

We were taught this at the tender age of six thanks to the BBC children's programme Words and Pictures. It was close to Halloween, and although not as popular back then as it is today, we were still all excited by the thought of witches flying over the village on their broomsticks. My best friend and I even stayed up until midnight to watch the spectacle of the witches, only to be bitterly disappointed. Not only were the streets not filled with the spirits of the departed visiting from the local graveyard, but there was not a witch to be seen. There followed the truth about the tooth fairy and also Father Christmas, but those are other stories of disappointment.

I was raised in a Christian family and attended a Church of England primary school. We were told that witches were horrid, nasty creatures that could turn you into a toad, or would kidnap children and cook them. Just the usual nightmarish stuff of children's story books. I was terrified of our next door neighbour who was a mysterious, short and slightly hunched old woman with long white hair. She seemed to always wear a long simple black dress and kept far too many cats. She didn't have a tooth to her name and spoke in such a thick country accent that even I, born and raised by locals, could not understand a word she said. I never saw her fly on a broomstick, but I was convinced she could if she had chosen to. I remember visiting the dark interior of her old cottage. It was sparsely decorated and the only room I went into had a large black range (large enough for a small child to fit in) and there was a large pot simmering on the stove. I clung to my mother's leg and refused to move for fear I'd be left behind. If this dear old widow had lived in the village a few hundred years earlier she was sure to have been burnt at the stake as she would have ticked most of the boxes on the witch hunters' check list. Plus, if anyone had asked that wide-eyed child hiding behind her mother, well, yes, I'd have condemned her too.

It wasn't till some 30 years later that I found myself far from my native village in Wiltshire, living in the Highlands of Scotland. I hadn't attended church for some time and felt uncomfortable with organised religion and people not putting into practise what they preached.

One Saturday afternoon, full of Starbucks caffeine, I found myself in the religious section of Borders bookshop. I felt like a naughty school child browsing through the Pagan titles when my hand fell to a copy of *The Way of the Hedge Witch* by Rae Beth. After reading a few lines I felt completely at home within those pages. The noise and busy shop faded into nothingness as I heard the words echo through my being, speaking to something deep within me. It was as though I was parched and dry and someone had given me crystal clear cooling water. When I resurfaced from those pages, the scene was somehow more colourful and vibrant than the one I'd left and I felt I had a direction. I practically flew to the cashier to pay with shaking hands. My family lost me for the next couple of days as I devoured the book.

Once I had started down that path I found I could not turn back. After being a Christian all my life I had my beliefs turned upside down by an afternoon spent curled up with a book about witchcraft. Witchcraft had cast its spell over me, pardon the pun.

While fuelled up with my enthusiasm for my new path, I wanted to devour books on the subject, I wanted to get stuck in straight away and perform rituals, set up an altar, change my style of clothing, get a tattoo... Well, maybe the last one had nothing to do with witchcraft, but I was bursting with a newfound energy and I wanted to fly let alone run before I could walk. Amazon was full of wonderful titles and I wanted to purchase each and every one. I soon discovered that my new found religion was not a cheap one if I wanted to fill my book shelves. The further I delved the more I found multiple websites full of magical supplies from candles to cauldrons, and you could get it all, at a price. This was when I realised witchcraft had become big business. A negative aspect of being a solitary witch, it seemed, was having to purchase your own equipment. There was no coven to share the cost with.

I didn't really want any part of the commercialism, being thrifty by nature I started to search out forums where

like-minded souls could gather together and exchange information, for free. Again there were plenty of sites full of such
opportunities, in fact too many. I had already set up a Facebook
account for myself, but decided to set one up as a solitary, and
hence The Highland Hedgewitch page was born. I half expect
taunts, posts condemning me to hell etc. However, I was pleas-
antly surprised. People seemed to like my page, and followers
arrived daily.

I found Facebook a place of acceptance and tolerance, and a
wealth of information and online covens, if I felt the need. If only
the witches of the past had access to such resources. If only
Gardner could see how far things had come the relatively short
space of time since he wrote his book, especially when you look
back through the mists of time to the earliest reports of witchcraft.

Due to my geographical location I found I was quite isolated.
I turned to the internet to find people similar to myself. They
were either hedge witches, solitaries or eclectic witches. Any one
of those names seemed to apply to myself. Working alone meant
I had no coven to report to, but then I had no support or
guidance either.

As a solitary witch, I was self-initiated. I followed Rae Beth's
instructions from my original purchase. I am blessed that living
where I do there are plenty of trees and wild open spaces where
I can be private and unobserved. I chose a beautiful oak tree
under whose beautiful protective branches I performed my own
initiation. It had to be an oak tree after my husband described
my newfound path as such. He remarked how Rae Beth's book
had been an acorn, which once planted firmly in my mind began
to take root. Then each month the roots grew stronger and
deeper. He commented on how the shoot pushed through the
darkness of confusion and rose up towards the light. How that,
too, grew stronger and with each new achievement another
branch grew.

Despite not having a coven's support and comradeship, I revel in being able to make my own rules, and follow my own needs. I'm fortunate that my immediate family are very supportive. My husband and teenage daughter join me when I celebrate the sabbats. They even join in when I perform spell work; my husband and I made a Hexenspiegel to repel negative energy and bad thoughts sent towards our home, and the mirror ball hangs in our front window now, catching the last of the light this autumn afternoon.

Being a solitary witch, it is easy to become eclectic. As I mentioned, I do follow my own rules, while always remaining true to the Wiccan Rede, "An Ye Harm None, Do What Ye Will". If what I'm doing feels right I believe the spell work I perform is stronger as a result. Belief, as in all religions, is important. If you don't believe in what you're doing, it is pointless. I am a great believer in the concept that what you send out will return to you threefold. I have in the past heard of those who wish to practise magic of a darker nature and, whilst everyone must follow their own path, I believe that you can only do yourself more harm in the process.

The weather may not be so kind up in the Highlands, but for me that is perfect. I love to work with the elements. However, wind is perhaps closest to my heart. Although it has a destructive side to its nature, it also has such freedom, such energy. I like to listen to it, to hear its stories, of journeys over mountains, through dense forests of ancient trees, of dancing over heathered moorland and sparkling streams. To stand with eyes closed and arms outstretched when the wind is at her wildest connects you to nature and the Goddess in a way I have found no other element can.

Although you wouldn't automatically think our cottage is any different to anyone else's when you walk in, there are certain tell-tale signs. I do have an altar set up in the kitchen. I have utilised a wide windowsill behind the sink; it is simple and has natural items upon it. The elements are marked. I have a tiger's eye hare to represent earth, a red candle for fire, seashells for water, and as air is my beloved element I have two items, incense and also a feather from my dear cockerel Tibby. My husband carved a chalice from oak and an athame from the same fallen tree. My husband and daughter are very accepting and should I wish to make a more elaborate show of my beliefs I doubt they would object. However, I am very aware that I share this cottage with them, and just because I am a witch does not mean they are. "Less is more" is a saying that has served me well in many situations.

My book shelves are a mish-mash of paperbacks with titles ranging from crystal magic to herb law. I'm afraid I'm still old school and the Kindle revolution hasn't quite arrived in our household. There are also various boxes of tarot and oracle cards there. I was fortunate enough to be gifted a set of cards by the wonderful Raven Grimassi and Stephanie Taylor. I felt drawn to this pack and believe that my readings are better with them as I have connected with them on a deeper level than some of my other packs. There are also Green Man and fairy oracle cards, all of which I use and adore. There are so many different packs available these days you are spoilt for choice. I know it's slightly stereotypical, "cross my palm with silver and I'll tell your fortune" type thing, but I see them as an integral part of my path, and have been known to use the cards to represent the God and Goddess on my altar.

Peoples' attitudes to different religions have become more relaxed. Paganism was the sixth largest religion in the UK in 2012. Sometimes, though, it seems things haven't progress that far. I work in a traditional old world profession by day and I wouldn't dream of bringing my beliefs into the office. I may have a couple of crystals on my desk, but they are discrete and the passerby wouldn't realise their significance. It is not that I am ashamed of who I am. However, I know when and where it is acceptable to fight my battles. I have members of my own family who struggle to understand my reasons for calling myself witch, and who still refuse to believe that I am anything but a Christian. I think once you have accepted who you are, and you take on the mantle of witch, you have to acknowledge that you will be called on to justify that title. People are generally curious; they want to know the ins and outs of what you do. Do you have a cauldron, black cat or, like Harry Potter, do you have a wand? At first I wasn't prepared for all the questions and would falter and want to withdraw as I felt I was under a spotlight. However, I understand now that it is just innocent curiosity, and most people have no idea what a 21st-century witch does. It is part of my path to educate when I can, in as gentle a way as possible.

When I think about how far I have walked along this path fully illuminated with acceptance and freedom, I begin to wonder why I was so drawn to it. A book spoke to something in me, it took hold of my imagination and my heart and I could never quite be the same after that. How different was it for the witches in the past? To be called that name would have meant certain death if you were caught practising. They were putting their lives on the line to be true to themselves, to walk a far scarier, darker and more dangerous path than I find myself walking today.

As a solitary witch I believe I have the best of both worlds, I can find companionship and support through social media and I have a wealth of information at my fingertips thanks to the internet and the smorgasbord of books written over the past 60 years. If only witches of the past could have had such support and resources. Though it does raise the question, if it has come this far out of the broom closet in the past 60 years, how will it develop and change within our lifetimes?

Highland Hedgewitch lives in the Scottish Highlands and runs the Highland Hedgewitch online community for sisters of the Hedge & Hearth.

Nature Witches

Rachel Patterson

Probably a strange term as most witches connect with nature, but there are some specific traditions that I would like to cover under the heading Nature Witches – Green Witchcraft, Kitchen Witchcraft and Faerie Craft. I don't believe that any of these pathways have strict, hard and fast rules as such, there is no rede or written-in-stone guideline, each person is an individual and everyone will walk a slightly different path and our spiritual journeys will be unique to us too.

Green Witchcraft

This is a fairly broad and general category sometimes used in association with Celtic Witchcraft, Kitchen Witchcraft and Faerie Craft and also in herbal magic. Herbalists who are not practising the art of Wicca occasionally call themselves Green Witches. There will also be crossovers which sometimes make labels restrictive. In my own pathway I take from various traditions – Wicca, Kitchen Witchcraft, Green Witchcraft, Hedge Witchcraft, Shamanism and Hoodoo to name a few, I take what works for me from each one and make it my own.

To me, Green Witchcraft is very much anchored in nature; a Green Witch will follow the turning of the Wheel and live very closely with Mother Earth and her seasons. A Green Witch will use all of nature's bounty for lotions, potions and spell work. It is a very natural and easygoing pathway, working in harmony with nature and the Elementals, but also working with the Divine in the form of the Goddess and the God. Energy is taken from the Earth, the plants, trees and herbs are used for health and healing work and a Green Witch will work very closely with the spirits of the plants, animals and landscape around them. The term

Green Witch is also sometimes used for those who follow the Pagan pathway, but make a priority of recycling, upcycling and generally reusing items and not wasting anything; a bit of an eco-warrior. A Green Witch will also prefer to make and use natural products for cleaning the house. A Green Witch is a naturalist (which leads them into being a botanist to a certain extent too), an herbalist and a healer.

Both Green Witches and Kitchen Witches will probably turn their hands to lotions and potions, not just of the magical kind, but also for the face and body and for medicinal uses. Soaps, bath salts and facial washes are all fairly straightforward to make and are lovely when made from natural ingredients and locally sourced plants and herbs.

Medicinal remedies are a little trickier in that you have to know exactly what plant you have just taken leaves from in the wild, because there are a few poisonous ones out there... and we don't want to be labelled as wicked witches! However, there are many medicinal uses for the everyday herbs and plants that we grow or the spices we have in our cupboards and that the Green or Kitchen Witch will utilise on a regular basis. A Green Witch will spend a lot of time foraging in the hedgerows and local woods for natural herbal ingredients.

Kitchen Witchcraft

The kitchen is the heart of many homes and it is here that a Kitchen Witch will spend most of her time, when she isn't out in the garden or hedgerows collecting herbs and wild plants.

There are a few similarities between a Green Witch and a Kitchen Witch... OK quite a lot in fact! A Kitchen Witch will work with nature, in tune with the seasons and the turning of the Wheel of the Year. A Kitchen Witch will also make lotions, potions and spells using natural items from plants, flowers and trees. The focus for a Kitchen Witch and a Green Witch is getting back to the basics and working with the bare essentials that nature provides and getting on with the job – no fuss, no theatrics and no grandeur. It's a hands-on, getting muddy (when necessary) back-to-basics kind of magic. A Kitchen Witch is also a naturalist, an herbalist and a healer in the same ways that a Green Witch is, but I believe a Kitchen Witch focuses her magic more around the food, the hearth and the ingredients. She (or he) is the wise woman/man.

A Kitchen Witch will also use the magic of herbs within her cooking. Each herb and edible plant has magical properties that can be added to ingredients and made into a meal or a drink. This can be adding a pinch of herbs and specific vegetables to make a soup for healing, for instance. A Kitchen Witch will also bring magic into the kitchen in many ways, such as stirring the pot deosil to bring positive energy into the food and will always add magic to any food that she is preparing or cooking.

When a Kitchen Witch has need of tools she will probably use whatever is to hand rather than have a set of specific magical tools, a wooden spoon becomes a wand, an old casserole pot makes a perfect cauldron and a vegetable knife is a good substitute for an athame.

There is not a lot of ceremony and pomp to a Kitchen Witch ritual. It will sometimes be slightly structured, but will go with the flow and whatever situation and space the witch is in will affect how the ritual proceeds. It might even be an impromptu ritual done on the spur of the moment in the middle of the kitchen! A Kitchen Witch might stick to the usual ritual set-up of casting a circle, but it will probably be done with her finger rather than an athame. The elements will be called in, energy raised and magic worked, but it will usually be done without any official magical tools although it may sometimes involve candles and herbs. But a Kitchen Witch might also just stand in their garden and call upon the elements to work with her/him, no circle casting, no candles, no tools, just the witch and the elements of nature helping to work the magic.

The kitchen will be the magical centre of a Kitchen Witch's world. My own kitchen has a small altar that I keep a tiny vase on. In this I put fresh flowers from the garden and I also have the elements represented in the form of a shell, a feather, a pebble and a red crystal. It is a focal point for me to connect with the divine when I work my magic when I am cooking, whether it is making dinner for my family or mixing up a potion. I also have a besom hung on the wall and witch balls from the ceiling (for protection). I even have some of the traditional Kitchen Witch dolls that originated in Eastern Europe. They are old, ugly, hag-type figures on broomsticks that fly across my kitchen ceiling. They were traditionally hung in a kitchen to bring luck to the household and avert culinary disasters. They were also believed to keep out harmful and negative energies. Yes, they do portray the witch as an old hag, but they are also a bit of history and a bit of fun; you have to have a sense of humour!

A Kitchen Witch and also a Green Witch will prefer to use vegetables and fruit that are in season and will cook in line with the turning of the Wheel, also using organic produce whenever possible (or affordable).

Magic can be worked in the kitchen even when performing the most mundane of tasks such as chopping vegetables. Release that pent-up frustration as you chop, let go of old habits and pent-up emotion as you wash away the dirt from your veggies, let the habits and negative energies wash away with the water. Sweeping is a wonderful way of clearing negative energies out of the house and magical floor washes are brilliant to bring in positive vibes. Any kneading, mixing or stirring may also involve a little bit of chanting, mine are never very poetic, but they do the trick.

The Sabbats are celebrated as they are in a lot of Pagan pathways, with focus on the food and plants of the season. Any excuse for cooking up a big celebration dinner!

And I know it sounds boring, but keeping the house clean is

also important, I think. For good energy to flow through the house you do really have to make like Snow White and keep the place clean and tidy. I can't focus properly if the house is untidy. In the same way a Green Witch does, a Kitchen Witch will also usually prefer to use organic and chemical-free cleaning products in the house, usually homemade versions of everything from toothpaste through to washing powder. Essential oils or dried flowers might also be added to the washing and cleaning products to add particular magical energies.

As a Kitchen Witch I work a lot with herbs and will use those in food for an added dash of magic, but also in magical workings such as medicine pouches or witches' bottles. The witch bottle is an ancient form of magic and the bottles made today are very similar to those used by our ancestors, although originally they were used to ward against witches!

A Kitchen Witch's house will most likely be jam packed with herbs hanging from the ceiling drying out and shelves filled with bottles and jars stuffed full of the herbs that have already been dried. I collect everything I can from the garden; herbs, of course, that grow in as many pots as I can fit into my small town garden, but also leaves, fallen sticks, seeds and petals from all the plants. Everything can be dried and stored away for future magical use. Intuition will play a huge part in the magical workings of a Kitchen Witch (and probably with a Green Witch too). They won't look up correspondences in reference books, they will go with their instinct and work with whatever herbs, crystals and colours that feel right and, of course, whatever materials they have to hand. If they don't have the herb or plant that a recipe requires (if they use a recipe at all) they will go with the ingredient they have in the cupboard that feels right as a replacement.

The garden is also important to a Kitchen Witch, even if it is a tiny one, as the witch will get all the ingredients needed for lotions and potions from it if possible. The garden is also a way to connect directly with nature and is so conveniently placed close to home! My own garden is my sanctuary. It is the place I go to relax, to release the stress of the day and to re-connect. My garden also has a bird table and lots of bird treats hanging from the tree. Feeding the birds is, for me anyway, a way of thanking the Goddess.

As a Kitchen Witch I personally work with deity, the Goddess and the Gods, but not all Kitchen Witches will do so. They may have that same focus, but they may also work with the ancestors, they may have a different religion or no religion at all.

You will probably also find that a Kitchen Witch is "crafty". I don't mean in a sneaky kind of way... well not all the time! But in a making things kind of way. A Kitchen Witch will often turn their hand to making medicine bags and pouches, witch bottles and jars, charms, amulets and talismans, all from natural easily obtainable items, and weave their own magic into the process. The house will be crammed full with protective bunches of herbs, a besom in the front porch turned bristles up to keep out unwanted guests, pendulums will be made from a hag stone dangling on a piece of string and seasonal decorations will all be made from natural items found in the local area. Yes I know we are headed to the vision of an old crone sitting in her rocking chair by a hearth fire doing her knitting and that is a traditional version of the witch. It may well be in some cases, but it will also have a modern twist of a witch sitting in a kitchen chair with a glue gun and a pile of pine cones making a Yule wreath!

I personally have several altars dotted about the house and they are a mixture of all the pathways I have walked and taken influence from. A Kitchen Witch altar will likely have lots of natural items on it. In fact it probably won't automatically be obvious that it is even an altar. It might just be a vase of flowers, some drift wood, a few sea shells, pebbles and some leaves, maybe even some candles. It will be seasonal; it may even have offerings of bread and mead or my personal offering of choice, cake.

Being a Kitchen Witch, for me anyway, involves a lot of folklore and folk magic, bringing in elements of gypsy magic too. It is an old and well worn pathway and I bet a lot of people work kitchen magic without even thinking about it.

Faerie Craft

I have worked with the world of the Fae since the very beginning of my journey, especially with the Elementals and the plant spirits. It can be challenging, the Fae can be pesky little critters, but Faerie Craft can also be very rewarding.

Once you get past the idea of faeries being all pink and glittery and flitting around with a pretty wand and get down to the *real* world of faerie, you will be amazed, enchanted and occasionally frustrated...

The word "fairy" or "faerie" comes from the ancient French "*faes*", derived from the Latin "*fata*". It was first apparently used around the 13th or 14th Century to describe spirit beings who had been central for hundreds of years in the oral folk tradition of many lands.

Faerie or fairy originally meant a state of enchantment or glamour, the power of illusion, reflecting the power of beings who might bring blessings or curses and ambivalence towards such beings. It was fear of angering the faery folk by speaking their name that led to their being given a variety of euphemisms that might, by a process of magic, attract only their benevolence.

There are faerie Gods and Goddesses, but the world of the Fae also holds Faerie Kings and Queens and their kingdom is one of wonder and inspiration.

Faerie Craft is a term that covers working with the faerie world and combining it with Wicca or witchcraft. There are various organised traditions within Faerie Craft, but I personally believe you can work your own faerie path and blend it with your own Pagan pathway very easily, as I have done.

The faerie world is large and complex and covers all sorts of

WITCHCRAFT TODAY ~ 60 YEARS ON

faerie folk of all shapes and sizes from tiny flower faeries up to huge great big trolls with all the various gnomes, pixies, sylphs, brownies and banshees in between.

I think of faeries as another aspect of the divine. They are there to help us if we ask and they are full of wisdom and knowledge. They also connect directly with nature and, in the case of the Devas and Elementals, are practically nature themselves.

If you look back through all the old faery tales and folk stories, the witch and the Fae have had a longstanding relationship. A witch has the ability to traverse between the worlds as do the Fae. They seem to have a mutual respect for each other. Faeries are also often linked with the sacred sites across the globe, all of which also have Pagan connections, so there must be something to it!

The world of faerie does not have laws as such, because each being from each race has its own personal code of conduct and a sense of self responsibility, one which perhaps humans could benefit from. Show a faerie respect and you shouldn't have a problem, but mess with them and you might find you have to deal with the consequences.

As a witch I work very closely with nature and all the plants, trees and flowers that Mother Earth provides, each of those plants has a plant spirit, a Deva or a Dryad (in the case of trees). These plant spirits are all part of the faerie world. The Devas are the plant architects, they oversee all areas of nature, whether it is a small town garden or a huge forest. Building a relationship with the Fae can help you to connect more directly with nature, I see it as a natural extension of my witchcraft.

What do you think you need in order to enter the faerie realm? You need to believe... believe that there is more out there than that which we can normally see.

The faerie realm is just that, a realm in its own right that runs alongside ours and every so often our worlds intersect. Media and literature would have us imagine all sorts of wonderful, mystical, faraway places to be the land of the Fae. But in actual fact the faery world is all around us. Nature provides us with the portals we just need to open our inner eyes to see them.

The faeries that I tend to work with most are the Elementals: Earth being the Gnomes, Air being the Sylphs, Fire being the Salamanders and Water the Undines. They are the raw, untamed energy of the elements; they are shape shifters and very powerful. Forget the garden gnome statue of a little man sitting holding a fishing rod, think more along the lines of an underground dwelling creature, very earthy and grounded. The Sylphs are probably the more archetypal faery; light and airy with gossamer wings. The Salamanders are not a lizard type creature, but more the flickering flames in the fire and the Undines are not like a cartoon mermaid sitting brushing her hair, they are water creatures. They are similar, but somehow more real and definitely not as cheesy! Freshwater Elementals are usually referred to as Undines and saltwater Elementals as mermaids or mermen. Mermaids have a history of singing beautifully to lure unsuspecting sailors to their deaths in their watery kingdoms...

I work with Elementals if I need the energy of a particular element. I have also led rituals where we have called upon the Elementals to lend their energies to the rite and it works very well.

Meditations and path workings to meet with members of the faerie world can be very rewarding and very enlightening, just be careful because the old tales of eating faerie food and being pixie led are true.

Once you start working with the Fae you will also find that they may leave you gifts and will most definitely visit you in your dreams to impart knowledge and insight.

Faerie altars are a good way to start your connection. They love sparkly things, tiny mirrors, sea shells, feathers and pretty flowers, in fact any natural objects you can find. The only thing I would advise against placing on a faerie altar is metal because they really don't react well to it. Offerings can be left on the altar too, as you would for as deity, but faeries like gifts that they can eat, such as honey or milk, and the offerings definitely need to be simple and bio-degradable. Show them respect and they will respect you.

Faerie Sabbats are the same timings as the Pagan Wheel of the Year. In fact these are the times of the year when it is easier to connect with the Fae.

Faerie Craft rituals are also similar to those of witchcraft and Wicca, you sweep the circle, cast the circle, call the elements, invoke the Faery King and Queen, raise power for healing or spell work and then close it all down in reverse. Faerie Craft is also a very good way to bring about healing.

The world of faerie is beautiful, mystical and magical, it can provide you with many insights, inspiration and healing, just be careful where you tread...

Rachel Patterson is High Priestess of the Kitchen Witch Coven and Team Leadership member of the Kitchen Witch School of Natural Witchcraft. She is the author of *Grimoire of a Kitchen Witch*, and three books in the *Pagan Portals* series – *Kitchen Witchcraft*, *Hoodoo* and *Moon Magic*. She lives in Portsmouth, UK.

Hekatean Witchcraft

Rick Derks

Hekate. Her titanic multi-armed form straddling the boundaries between the worlds. Her head rests among the empyrean heights, and her feet within the darkest reaches of the chthonic underworld. Six arms outstretched, blazing torches held aloft, burning the fires of purest wisdom. Six sets of burning eyes, affixed in turn within three animal formed heads, the snake, horse, and dog, pierce your defenses and gaze into your inner soul. She wears an armor of writhing serpents over her scaled torso. The entirety of nature is suspended upon her back, and virtue's flow erupts from her hip. Choirs of angels and hordes of restless spirits bow to her. The scent of burning dog flesh permeates the air. A pair of golden lions flank her sides. The howls of daemon dogs mournfully pierce the night, comingled with the rattling of chains.

Above is an image of the goddess Hekate as she has been portrayed in *The Chaldean Oracles* and numerous other sources, and has appeared to me the few times she has deemed to appear to me. Whether just another in the latest cycles of Pagan fads, or a true potent force come back to the world, one thing remains: Hekate is a goddess whose name is on everyone's lips these days. While on the rise for decades, Hekate's worship has really bloomed in the past few years. Much of this is due to the diligence and devotion of her current worshippers. Many books have been published about her recently, and organizations such as the Covenant of Hekate have brought her into the forefront of people's consciousness and made her accessible to seekers once more.

I can think of a few reasons for her current popularity. In my own workings with her, I've come to see her as a Goddess of the Lost. She's the torchbearer. She guides our way. I personally think she tends to reach out to those of us who are lost on our spiritual path and feeling around in the dark. At least that's how she came to me. I'd wager to say there are a lot of us out there who fit that bill. She tends to take in those wild souls who exist on the liminal outskirts of spirituality, not really fitting into any accepted paradigm or tradition. Spiritual outsiders as it were. We are her children. For some she may remain their goddess forever, for others she may serve her role as crossroads goddess, aiding transition and guiding them to the next phase of their life, whatever that may be. One thing is certain, though, she leaves her mark on all of those whom she touches.

Hekatean Witchcraft

What exactly is Hekatean Witchcraft? This is simply witchcraft or sorcery which primarily concerns itself with the mysteries of Hekate. The term is not without its challenges. First off, I do not want to convey that this is a specific tradition, either ancient or modern, initiatory or otherwise. There is no specific tradition one can point to that is "The Hekatean Witchcraft Tradition". The witchcraft of Hekate is a thread that runs deep into history and has many modern expressions ranging from the strict reconstructionist stance to the fairly eclectic. Gather five devotees together and ask what Hekatean Witchcraft is, and you may get seven different responses.

Furthermore, a distinct trait among the Hekatean Witches I've found is fierce individuality. Hekate is, after all, a goddess of liminality and those who dwell on the fringe, whom I call "boundary people", often tend to do things their own way and own style. Hekate's devotees often tend to be outcasts from the traditional scene in one way or another, and usually this is by choice. Most I have met have been unsatisfied with traditional forms of magic or religion, or straddle the boundaries between multiple traditions. This can cause for some quite different methods of worship and magic, and often resulting in heated debate and discussion amongst practitioners.

Thus there are as many individual forms of Hekatean Witchcraft as there are Hekatean Witches! Anyone trying to sell you a one true way of Hekatean Witchcraft should be looked at with suspicion. That being said, however, there is a long history of Hekate's association with witchcraft and new threads based on these ancient traditions are being woven back together even today. Hekate's modern worship is a *living* tradition, rooted in history, yet it is changing and growing today as you read this. Each new devotee puts their own spin on her worship.

First we must examine her historical tradition. To work with Hekate without knowing the traditions behind her would be to do both yourself and her a disservice. It is always good to be grounded and educated in tradition before you begin to spin your own threads. I will offer a starting point on this, but it is best to seek out the traditional sources on your own to ground yourself in her long history and past.

A Brief History of Hekate's Witchcraft

The history of the goddess we know as Hekate spans back thousands of years and an exhaustive exploration of that history is beyond the scope of this chapter. Thus, I will be touching on some of the main aspects here so that we may have a common framework with which to explore her modern mysteries. I do urge you, though, to read some of the historical references to conduct your own investigation into her origins.

Hekate's worship can be divided into three main stages. Her ancient cult, her role in the Hellenistic era, and her role in the later Chaldean oracles. Although mainly known for her appearance in Greek religion, it is thought she is most likely an import from Asia Minor and the land which is now known as modern day Romania, where remnants of her traditions still appear. From here her cult likely comes to us from that of an archetypical mother goddess, and early images associated with her, such as the "Anatolian snake goddess", may be her cognates. Although there is little historical precedence for it, R. Lowe Thompson suggests that the ancient cult of Hekate may have developed in tandem with the ancient cult of the Horned God, which is an intriguing prospect. Here he theorizes that these two cults began at roughly the same point, but were taken in different directions by different cultures. Unfortunately, there is very little for us to go on here other than to suggest that Hekate was not a native to Greek mythology, much like Dionysos, with whom she is often said to work closely.

Other tantalizing hints to her ancient origins are her status within Greek mythology as a Titan. The Titans were the original primordial power with whom the classical Hellenistic gods waged war to wrest control of the world, imprisoning the majority of them in the deep Tartarus. Hekate was said to be instrumental in helping the gods against the other Titans, and thus was granted dominion by Zeus over the land, sea, and sky. Additionally, one of her traditional sacrifices was that of black dogs or ewes, burnt in pits in the ground. This was a type of sacrifice that was usually reserved for foreign deities. Her status as a Titan suggest a pre-Olympic pantheon origin.

By the Hellenistic era, around 430BC, her cult was established in Athens, which is where we get most of the information we know about her. Here the earliest known images of Hekate took the place of Hekataions, which were poles set at crossroads with three masks affixed to them to protect and guide travelers. These were often found next to herms, or stacks of stones dedicated to Hermes, thus an early connection between the two. By the late Hellenistic era, she was transformed from the protective and apotropaic mother goddess to being primarily associated with necromancy and ghosts, often having a retinue of the dead following her.

It was here that she may have gained her associations with witchcraft. Here we see mostly chthonic associations attributed to her. Her connections to witchcraft increased, becoming the patroness of witches and necromancers, a reputation which followed her well into the Middle Ages, as evidenced by her depiction by Shakespeare in Macbeth. Also, we see this association in the mythology of Medea the sorceress. Hekate was said to be the patron and possibly even the mother of Medea, and is credited as the source of her power. A prayer referencing Medea's acknowledgment of this is found in Ovid's *Metamorphosis*:

> O night, faithful friend of mysteries; and you, golden stars and moon, who follow the fiery star of day; and you, Hecate, goddess with threefold head, you know my designs and come to strengthen my spells and magic arts; and you, earth, who offer your potent herbs to magi; and airs, winds, mountains, streams, and lakes, and all you woodland gods, and all you gods of the night: Be present now.

The idea of ancient witches dedicating themselves to Hekate is not without its controversy however. Jacob Rabinowitz in his book *The Rotting Goddess* suggests that there were in fact no ancient sorcerers calling on Hekate, and that this is a romantic literary invention. Whether this is true or not is a matter of controversy in itself, but regardless of what may have happened in the past, the fact remains that now quite a few witches and sorcerers call her patron!

One central rite in the cult of Hekate during this period, which persists to the modern day, is known as the Deipnon, or Hekate's supper. This takes place on the dark of the moon, the last night of the lunar month when no portion of the moon can be seen in the sky. A meal is left at the crossroads, consisting of fish, cheese, bread, onions, and honey, and is placed without looking back behind you. This is considered Hekate's meal alone. This is a central rite to the cult of Hekate, and many modern devotees practice it today, linking them to her devotees in the past.

As a personal antecedent, I once offered such supper to her during the month of October. As I walked off, I heard the rattling of chains so strongly I turned, startled, to look behind myself, expecting to see an escaped, chained dog charging me. As I turned, breaking the rule, the sound ceased (I trust she has forgiven me the slight).

By the late 2nd century AD, *The Chaldean Oracles* were being circulated in the ancient world. These were a set of doctrines which where the precursors to modern Neo-Platonism and later Hermeticism, said to be written by "The Two Julians", a father-and-son team who served as mediums for its dictation. In *The Chaldean Oracles*, Hekate is seen as an intermediary between the first and second fathers, the creator gods and architects of the universe. Here she is equated with the world soul or *animus mundi*, and takes on a much more empyrean role, flanked with lions and having all of nature suspended on her back, with virtue flowing from her hip. She is also in command of a whole host of "angels", in contrast to her hordes of underworld spirits in ages past. Hekate is thus elevated from a purely chthonic deity, to one who is a light bearer and queen of the heavens. Thus she has retained both of these roles to the present day. In keeping with her role as the Chaldean world soul, Rabinowitz suggests that she is the word tree itself.

No treatise on Hekatean Witchcraft would be complete without discussing her role in the *Greek Magical Papyri* (PGM). The PGM is a collection of texts, spells, and rituals taken from the period between the 2nd Century BC to the 5th Century AD. It is fragmentary and highly syncretic in nature, merging Greek, Egyptian, Babylonian, and Christian influences and traditions. Hekate and Helios are the two deities who are mentioned the most in this group of spells, often accounting for the two being put alongside one another today. While most of the spells within it may sound archaic and somewhat arcane, the words of power and invocations found within are often used today in connection with Hekate for modern purposes. It is a treasure trove for those wishing to enhance their sorcery and it's my belief that anyone who wishes to engage in Hekatean-related sorcery should have a copy on their night stand.

Hekatean Witchcraft in the Present Day

In the present day, Hekatean Witchcraft is an umbrella term, much like the term "Traditional Witchcraft" itself, which encompasses a wide variety of traditions ranging from the strictest reconstructionist perspective to the greatly eclectic. Due to this fact it can be hard to present an accurate picture of just what a Hekatean Witch is! In fact even the word "witch" is often the source of much disagreement amongst Pagan folk these days.

The fact is that Hekate is invoked not just by those would normally be labeled as witches these days, but equally by many other types of magic practicing folks such as ceremonial magicians, sorcerers, and even Druids! Her dual nature as a chthonic deity and a celestial light bringer make her well sought after by those whose affinity lies with solar and lunar currents of magic alike.

Likewise, her devotees run the gambit between those interested in just devotional worship, those interested in working with her for magic and sorcery, and the entire spectrum in between. Which begs the question... Who exactly can we call a Hekatean Witch? Unfortunately the answer to this question is not an easy one, and coming up with a definition that everyone will agree upon is probably downright impossible, and certainly outside the range of this writers' ability.

The Hedge Witch chanting wildly and ecstatically to Hekate underneath the full moon in the rural Midwest US could be considered a Hekatean Witch. The adherent to Hellenisimos somewhere in the UK, offering Khernips and observing the

Deipnon with traditional Orphic hymns may consider themselves a Hekatean Witch. The lodge magician, enacting a full ritual rite to Hekate may be a Hekatean Witch. A Wiccan who worships Hekate on the full moon may be a Hekatean Witch.

The variety is stunning to behold. One can only point at common threads running between them, the worship of and devotion to Hekate herself. To illustrate this, let's take an example of two different perspectives I myself have been involved with. The International Covenant of Hekate founded by Sorita D'Este is an organization that is not witchcraft focused, yet caters for many who practice witchcraft with Hekate. They primarily work with Hekate in a more traditional manner, exploring her role as the World Soul as espoused in *The Chaldean Oracles*. Here theurgy, or ritual involving connection to the divine, is a skill which is developed and focused on for the purpose of achieving henosis (divine union) with Hekate. Here the traditional hymns and offerings to Hekate are honored, yet new practices are developed by the collective membership to continue to further and evolve her worship. It mainly has a devotional focus, yet many of its members practice thaumaturgy as well, all within a traditional framework, reworked through a modern day lens.

In contrast, at the opposite end of the spectrum one would find the Primal Craft tradition, a fully realized Traditional Witchcraft tradition based on the writings and gnosis of Mark Alan Smith. This tradition takes the opposite approach, and instead of working with Hekate in her classical role, it instead sees her as a deeply primal force and the central figure of its pantheon, and pairs her along with Lucifer and Belial. The main goal of this tradition is to attain alchemical transformation of the soul through journey to the qlippothic realms and interaction with these witchgods. While it may seem highly unorthodox to place Hekate next to Lucifer and Belial, one need only read *Aradia: Gospel of the Witches* to find clues to Hekate's connections to Lucifer (hint: Hekate is often associated with Artemis). Indeed many Luciferians place Hekate in their pantheon, as her light-bringer nature makes her an obvious choice in this pairing.

It is interesting to note, that even though evoking the same goddess, calling to Hekate through either of these frameworks will yield a very different feeling experience, the poised and classical Hekate compared to a primal, almost feral Hekate, further highlighting the variety of experience awaiting the would be Hekatean Witch.

These represent only two ways Hekate can be worked with. Indeed, many even choose to work with her in a personal way that defies any need for further labeling. In fact, one might say that in recent years a current has been emerging in which the worship of Hekate is becoming its own religious egregore, independent of outside traditions. This current brings together many people of different backgrounds under her banner. This is not to say, however, that "anything goes" when working with Hekate, only that in my experience and observation she is quite liberal with whom she chooses to work with. Some traditional ways to work with her will be described below.

Working with Hekate in the Modern Day

Let's explore together some of the ways that someone new to Hekatean worship might go about working with her and immersing themselves in her modern current. The first thing you will want to decide is if you wish to work with her alone or with other gods. Many choose to eventually shed all of the other deity connections they have and devote themselves solely to Hekate, such is the strong devotion she evokes in those she calls to her side. If you choose this option you may find yourself in a very fulfilling yet demanding relationship with this goddess, a type of Hekatean Henotheism. Often devotees find this option is chosen for them, as they begin to lose "signal strength" with all other gods while her influence grows.

Another question that arises to new devotees is the decision between hard and soft polytheism. While Hekate seems often-times cognate with deities of other pantheons, many (but not all) of her worshippers tend to take a hard polytheist stance, which dictates she is herself and only herself, not a mask of, say Cerridwen or The Morrigan. She is thought of as an independent entity of her own accord, not a manifestation of the "Great Goddess" (though syncretisms do exist, confounding the issue further). If you decide to pursue this line of thought you may wish to contemplate the doctrine of polycentric polytheism, which states that all gods are contained within all others. Thus you may find that the perceived connections between Hekate and other goddesses of different pantheons may not be the fact that they are all the same, but you are viewing that aspect of that goddess within Hekate.

Additionally, and in modern times, she can be paired success-fully with other gods. Notice this differs and contrasts with Wiccan traditions where a goddess is paired with a consort. Hekate can pair with male gods, but conventional wisdom on the matter states that she is never a consort (she is in fact considered a virgin goddess). However, she is well known for working together closely with Hermes, Dionysos, Zeus, and Helios just to name a few.

Next you may wish to start examining her primary historical sources for clues to her worship, some suggestions given below. Her traditions span thousands of years into the past, creating deep *established* pathways with which to contact her in a way that she is used to. Often someone new will benefit from keeping these traditions. A rule of thumb is don't be afraid to change something, but know why you are doing it. Do not just do it because "it feels right". A chef often learns to cook a dish thoroughly before putting their own spin on it. In this way don't confuse authenticity with validity. Ancient traditions may be authentic, but this does not confer their validity, and modern traditions can be just as valid and spiritually fulfilling as the old, if approached from a place of wisdom and respect. One such way would be to use Vox Magicae. One method that is often used to invoke Hekate is the use of the Ephesian letters. The Ephesian letters are *askion, kataskion, lix, tetrax, damnameneus,* and *aision*. These are words found in a shrine to Artemis at the shrine of Ephesia, but a number of these words are used in the PGM in a charm PGM LXX.12. The barbaric words used in this passage are *"Askei Kataskei Eron Oreon Ior Mega Samnyer Baui Phobantia Semne..."* These words are often chanted by Hekate devotees as a way to connect with the goddess. It is often used in the form of saying the phrase *"Askei Kataskei Eron Oreon Ior Mega Samnyer Baui"* three times, followed by saying the final words *"Phobantia Semne"*. The exact translation of the words in unknown, though it is thought that each has a significance to Hekate and one of her mysteries.

You might also wish to recite her Orphic hymn, given here in both Greek and English:

Einodian Hekatên, klêizô, Trihoditin Erannên,
Ouranian, Chthonian, te kai Einalian, Krokopeplos.
Tymbidian, Psychais Nekyôn meta bakcheuosan,
Perseian, Philerêmon, agallomenên elaphoisi.
Nykterian, Skylakitin, amaimaketon Basileian.
Thêrobromon, Azôston, aprosmachon Eidos echousan.
Tauropolon, Pantos Kosmou Klêidouchon, Anassan,
Hêgemonên, Nymphên, Kourotrophon, Ouresiphoitin.
Lissomenos, Kourên, teletais hosiaisi pareinai,
Boukolôi eumeneousan aei kecharêoti thymôi.

Hekate Einodia, Trioditis, lovely dame, of earthly, watery, and celestial frame, sepulchral, in a saffron veil arrayed, pleased with dark ghosts that wander through the shade; Perseis, solitary goddess, hail! The world's key-bearer, never doomed to fail; in stag's rejoicing, huntress, nightly seen, and drawn by bulls, unconquerable queen; Leader, Nymphe, nurse, on mountains wandering, hear the suppliants who with holy rites thy power revere, and to the herdsman with a favouring mind draw near.

The recitation of this hymn has been used for centuries to invoke Hekate. Think of it as a kind of phone number that hones in on her and gets her attention. While using the English form is perfectly acceptable, many Hekateans devote themselves to learning the Greek version as a devotional exercise. Chanting this in its original tongue can be a thing of beauty and consciousness enhancing experience. Together with the Vox Magicae above, and an offering of incense, one would have a strong start in getting her attention and working with her. Follow this up with a heartfelt prayer of your own, in your own words.

Also, this could be combined with a Hekate's supper on the dark moon. Ideally this would be performed at a crossroads, leaving an offering of fish, eggs, bread, and garlic without looking back afterwards. However, not all of us are lucky enough to have access to such a place where our activities would go unnoticed, so your own ritual area or backyard would work just as well. I have seen some enterprising sorcerers create their own crossroads indoors by taking dirt from a natural crossroads and pouring it on a dish or plaque in a cross form to generate a portable indoor crossroads that works symbolically just as well.

Speak to her from your heart, approach her with reverence and without hubris, root yourself in tradition, and in time add your own unique stamp on her worship. In nomine de Hekate.

Rick Derks runs *Primal Craft*, a website dedicated to the Witchcraft of Hekate.

Bibliography

Betz, Han D. *The Greek Magical Papyri in Translation: Including the Demotic Spells: Texts Volume 1.* Chicago. University of Chicago Press. 1992

Butler, Edward, P. *Essays on a Polytheistic Philosophy of Religion.* Phaidra Editions. 2012

Johnston, Sarah Iles. *Hekate Sotiera.* Atlanta, Georgia. Scholars Press. 1990.

Majercik, Ruth. *The Chaldean Oracles.* 1998

Michev, Georgi. *Thracian Magic Past and Present.* London, UK. Avalonia. 2012

Ogdem, Daniel. *Greek and Roman Necromancy;* Princeton, New Jersey. Princeton University Press. 2001

Rabinowitz, Jacob. *The Rotting Goddess.* Autonomedia. 1998

Ronan, Stephen. *The Goddess Hekate.* Hastings, UK. Chthonios Books. 1992

Smith, Mark Alan. *The Queen of Hell.* Finland. Ixaxaar Occult Literature. 2010

Thompson, Lowe, R. *History of the Devil: The Horned God of the West.* London. 1992

The Egyptian Magical Tradition

Martha Gray

The Egyptian magical tradition is still followed today, though those who practice it are not as numerous as those who follow the various witchcraft traditions. It has in some periods, such as the 1990s, gained interest due to the trends of the time.

The study and practice of Egyptian magic is quite varied, depending on which tradition within the Egyptian system is followed. Egypt had an empire lasting over three thousand years, besides its pre dynastic societies. Like all cultures through time, changes were made to match the political climate and social structures of the era. However, no matter what the time frame, or which tradition the modern practitioner follows, magic and mythology played a very important role in the daily lives of those living in Ancient Egypt. That tradition has survived and is practised to this present day.

If you want to be a part of the Egyptian tradition, it is essential to do your homework and study the history. Yes, there is a lot of it, but those who understand the evolution of Egypt's history and the complexity of the mythology as well as how it developed over time with the help of the priests who succeeded each other, are best enabled to work with the magical tradition.

Predynastic Egypt, 5000BCE to 3050BCE, was not a unified country at all, but had 42 nomes, or regions, with their own deities and kings. The dominant feature of the time, however, was a split between the north and the south, with rivalry between the two main factions, one following Horus and the other Set.

Set's cult centre was believed to be in Upper Egypt in the south and appears to have had dominance over the area around the eastern delta and Libya, as well as over all classes including the ruling elite. Upper Egypt was symbolized by the red low crown (deshret), the symbols of which were the papyrus plant and the cobra goddess Wadjett. There is a lot of evidence from archaeological findings to suggest Naquada, on the bank of the Nile, was the earliest settlement in Egypt. It is also thought to have been the origin of Set worship. It was there, around 5000 BCE, where villages were established and the Baderian emerged. The beginning of irrigation of the Nile Valley started around 4500BCE, which we call Naquada 1. Around 3500BCE-3300BCE came Naquada 11, with the Gurzeam. It continued to grow and was favoured by the high-born families, becoming a centre of importance. The first rulers, who were the Thinites, were believed to come from somewhere near Abydos.

At that time Set was depicted in form as the Set animal. This creature has no particular resemblance to a living animal. The figure is that of the body of a dog with a forked tail, the head has a long snout with the ears wedged and pointed. Though some would say the animal is close to an armadillo, jackal or boar, a more common description is to liken it to a dog.

He is a god of great antiquity whose timeline may go well back into pre-historic tribal worship. Set (Sutekh) was a storm and weather god. In predynastic times he was looked upon as the adversary to Horus, who was the god of the sky by day, while Set was the god of the sky by night. They had become two sides of one deity. In a period when two sides were fighting one another over land, the beliefs about Set and Horus reflected that conflict.

As time went on, Set became unfairly demonized. The ruling priesthoods could not eradicate a deity with so much power embedded deeply into the subconscious of the country's inhabitants. He became the adversary. He became the sibling of Osiris, Isis, Horus and Nephthys, and became the adversary of Osiris as the Osirian cult took off. He was the murdering brother and lord of the deserts and ruler of chaos.

In the Middle Kingdom, Set's power was still well understood and he became the defender of Re, who stood on his Manjet, the boat of millions of years, that sailed through the night sky. Set was the god who defeated Apep, the serpent god, so Re could emerge at dawn to bring the life-giving sun to the world.

Lower Egypt, in the North, was symbolized by a flowering lotus and the tall white crown (hedjet), which was represented by the vulture goddess Nekhbet. For Lower Egypt, Horus seemed to be the dominant deity and Set's rival.

Horus was a sky god who was depicted in the guise of a falcon. He is a god of great antiquity. A myth from the early tradition states that when Atum Re emerged from the primordial waters, Horus was the source of life and death and the rain and celestial fire. He was there at the beginning, when nothing else was. The form of Horus gave light to the darkness. He became Re's visual solar symbol as Re Herekhte and the symbol of kingship. He had many names as the myths were combined from the adversary of Horus, to his brother. He was given the name of Horus the Elder as the brother of Isis and Osiris and later Horus the Younger as the son of Isis, as the myths became blurred in later dynasties. His followers, unlike Set's followers with an established capital and grouped peoples, probably emerged from outer nomes of Lower Egypt.

Anyone who studies the Egyptian magical tradition and wishes to take the old primitive path would have to wade through the layers of myths and dual-named deities and take each energy to its primal level to understand each one from the core origins. The predynastic peoples were most likely stellar worshippers and in touch with the core forces of nature. Horus and Set were the dominant deities of the times, but if we look at them from a magnified point of view, stripping the trappings of myth away, we can see the true characteristics. Working with the forces in their pure forms we get to really appreciate the great power of Egypt.

In 3250BCE came the unification of the two lands. This

brought the red and white crowns together under one Pharaoh, Narme or Mens, who defeated King Scorpion. During Dynasty 1 and 11, Memphis became the capital. They created the symbol of the double crown and adopted this to try to create a more stable land. However, there was still conflict between the two rivals and it appears that Set's followers gained supremacy for a while with the Pharaoh Sekhemib putting aside his Horus name in favour of his Set name.

Pharoahs always had more than one name, especially at their coronation, when they adopted a new one that was fitting to their deity. As Pharaoh, they were identified with the god and therefore believed to be the incarnation of the sun, Horus. In their funerary rights, which at that time were exclusive to the Pharaoh, they ascended to the stars on a ladder that was held on each side by Horus and Set and became one among the heavens.

The Old Kingdom, which began in 2686BCE and lasted six dynasties until 2181BCE, saw the great age of the master craftsman and their tomb buildings. It was this age that gave us the pyramids that can still be seen up and down the country. There are about 80 pyramids in varying states across the country. The best known and preserved are the pyramids at Gizza. The pyramids were designed by the astronomer priesthood as an aid for the Pharaoh to ascend to the heavens. These structures were constructed with the alignment of the stars in mind. There is evidence that the Great Pyramid and the two lesser ones at Gizza were built in line with the three stars of Orion's belt. Calculations of the celestial bodies at the time of building would suggest this is so. It shows the importance of a stellar connection with magic and religious beliefs and ceremonies. In those times, people did not have problems with visibility of the stars due to light pollution as we do today. The skies must have been a wonder to behold.

The priesthood also composed the *Pyramid Texts*, the first of the funerary books. These included the spells necessary for the

Pharaoh to attain afterlife among the stars. In the earlier dynasties it was believed that when the Pharaoh was buried, everything he would need to enjoy the afterlife should go with him. That included all slaves, servants and any other body he would need. By this time they had come to realize this was a waste of resources and good workers and slaves were hard to find and train, so in their place they created ornamental images of all the slaves and workers instead, as a representation.

By Dynasty 4 the priests and nobles of the higher government were getting richer and started to gain more power. It is then that we start to see the collapse of the older religious systems and the country falling into a state of unrest. By the first intermediate period of 2181BCE to 2040BCE, during Dynasties 7 and 8, the country was in turmoil.

It was not until what we now call the Middle Kingdom, 2040BCE, and the 11th Dynasty, that the country settled down again. The capital had moved to Thebes. For two dynasties until 1782BCE, Egypt again had a more stable society. During this period they had a more intellectual outlook, which was evident in their literature and they were more artistically creative and more lavish. The priesthood continued to grow in importance and power, taking more control from the ruling elite.

The type of worship emerging at this time was solar, rather than the former stellar worship. During this period, the Pharaoh was identified as Amun Re, the great solar deity. The priesthood also began to weave new myths and combine male and female deities as consorts. This included Ptah, the craftsman creator god, and Sekhmet, who was the goddess of war, famine and destruction. Their son was Neferatum, who rose from the primordial waters on the blue lotus and was said initially in the *Pyramid Texts* to be the blue lotus where the sun rises in the morning. This was the symbol of perfection. Initially, though, he was a local deity of Buto in the Nile Delta. He was originally the son of the cobra Goddess Wadjet, who could take lionine form.

This was to create the concept of family harmony and unity, so everyone could identify with them. It was also to install a sense of morality into the people.

The priesthood composed the *Coffin Texts*, which were an extension of the funerary utterances of the *Pyramid Texts*. As the name suggests, these were written on the interior of coffin lids and tomb walls of the deceased to aid them in the afterlife. The chance to ascend into the afterlife was now not just available to the ruling elite, but to anyone who could afford it or had the equipment.

It was during this period we started to see the Egyptians making great advances in medicine as they continued intellectual learning. From these seeds grew the greatest medical practitioners of the ancient world. This was further excelled in the New Kingdom as they advanced further.

It was also the time when we start to see the emergence of the Osirian cult. Osiris was originally thought to be a local vegetation god who had gained supremacy with the cult of Isis by the Late Kingdom onwards.

From 1782BCE-1570BCE, the second intermediate period saw the weakening of Egypt with the invasion of the Hyksos princes. Although central government was intact, the princes ruled in regions of Egypt. However, Thebes was still held as the centre and the areas from Elephantine to Abydos were still kept relatively unscathed. An uneasy truce between the Egyptian princes and the Hyksos remained until Ahmose, the last ruler of the 17th Dynasty, drove the Hyksos out.

The New Kingdom, 1870-1293BCE, was seen in by Ahmose who founded Dynasty 18. During this time Egypt enjoyed its greatest period of advancement and expansion. It not only saw its first female pharaoh, Queen Hatshepsut, 1898 BCE-1483BCE, but also gave us Pharaohs with great military might, such as Tuthmoses III, who has been called the Napoleon of the ancient world. Tuthmoses III also began a program to restore many ancient structures as well as building new ones. The most famous Pharaoh was Ramesses II. He was an expert soldier and did everything on a grand scale, including great buildings and statues, some of which still survive today.

The principle deity, Amun, expanded even more in popularity and the priesthood controlled much of the lands. Most of the Gods of the Old Kingdom still survived, but were combined and woven into a mythology that introduced newer deities which rose from older regional nomes such as Mut, the consort to Amun. Mut is the Egyptian name of "mother". She had become identified as the mother of Pharaoh. Her form is a slim woman with a headdress combining the feathers of a vulture with the upper and lower crowns of Egypt. Although she was identified with the vulture she was also identified with the lioness, and bore the name Mut-Sekhmet in her protective warrior mode, as well as with the softer side of the female nature as the cat which can be stroked, as Mut-Bastet. The power and psychological influence of the old deities such as Sekhmet could never be wiped from the subconscious of Egyptian society, which is why they combined attributes with those they were compatible with.

During this period Amenhotep IV, better known as Akhenaten, 135BCE-1334BCE, introduced monotheism with worship of the sun disk Aten. According to the *Chronicle of the Pharaohs*, Akhenaten was a great thinker and philosopher. His father had recognized the growing power of the priesthood and wanted to curb it. Akhenaten went much further.

He even went as far as to move the capital to what is now el-Amarna. This was due to conflict with those who still supported Amun. On the death of Akhenaten, his name was scrubbed from the monuments. In the short reign of Smenkhkare 1336BCE-1334BCE, power was restored to the capital and the traces of Akhenaten's name were removed from any monument or writings as a disgrace to Egyptian society.

During the Third Intermediate Period, 1069BCE-525BCE,

Egypt began a downward spiral from which it would never recover. The country faced bankruptcy around 1000BCE and it was no longer a closed land of the god kings. Influences from the outside world started to filter in. There was turmoil throughout the land with varying rulers. The throne was sat upon by Nubian princes from 747BCE. The Persians came in 525BCE and took control of the country, but also sacked and destroyed temples and libraries where much ancient wisdom was stored.

In the late period, 525BCE-332BCE, Egypt was controlled by the Persians. The last Egyptian Pharaoh, Necatanebo, could not win the country back and went into exile in Nubia. Alexander the Great drove the Persians out in 332BCE. He was seen as a saviour by the people. The Greeks had a great love of wisdom and tried to collect and rebuild the knowledge of Egypt's past. Some of the knowledge was badly interpreted due to language barriers and missing fragments of information.

During this time the cults of Isis and Osiris, who were gods of old, were integrated into the great funerary cult of the time to offer salvation to everyone judged by the feather of Ma-at in the Hall of Judgement to have lived good lives. They were then permitted to pass into the afterlife of Amenti. *The Book of Going Forth by Day*, which was renamed *The Book of the Dead*, was an instructional manual and a series of spells on passing safely through the underworld. This new form of beliefs was developed with the changes of the time and was a more devotional cult of the sacrificial god, based around the mythological background of the gods, the death of Osiris at the hands of his brother Set and the resurrection of the god of the underworld. Osiris had gained the title of God of the Rains and the life-giving force that had overshadowed Set and sent him into a villainous role. Osiris was seen as being responsible for the waters of the life-giving Nile. This inundation, which happened every year and which the Egyptians depended on for food and water, had come under the role of Osiris. He ruled with his sister, Isis, who had become the

Queen of the Gods.

The Romans invaded in 32BCE and, only a few years afterwards, the religion of Christianity began to appear in Egypt. The
framework for this was based on the death cult of Osirian
worship.

What is Egyptian magic in our modern day? It is all of the
above. It is only in recent times we have been able to understand
this ancient empire and its peoples. With detailed archaeological
digs and modern technology, such as carbon dating, X-rays and
deep scanning of objects and places, we are piecing this colossal
jigsaw together.

The study and practice of Egyptian magic in our current
society is varied. There are schools out there that offer teaching
aimed at a particular tradition or group of deities. There are
many out there who are attracted to the cult of Isis, which in
modern times and with the advance of feminism is part of the
trend towards worshipping female energies. The mythology of
the Theban Osirian Isis cult and the identification with the deities
and their structured family can also be related to by those in our
current climate. The Osirian family were the children of Nut and
Geb. There were five: Osiris, Isis, Nephthys, Set and Horus (the
Elder).

Osiris from this mythological concept came to Egypt and
taught people how to grow crops and grapes. He also bought
justice to the lands. He decided to travel the world to spread his
teachings. When he came back, Set who was jealous of him,
decided to have him murdered and scattered the parts of his
body all over Egypt. Isis, who was deep in mourning, hunted
down all the parts so the body could be resurrected to bear her a
child. With the help of Thoth's magic she managed to conceive a
boy, Horus (the younger).

Nephthys was spouse to Set. On Osiris's death she separated
from him. While Set was represented as the desert and barren
lands and Osiris the fertile Nile, Nephthys was that land

inbetween the two. She was seen as being the goddess between the worlds of the living and the dead, the goddess of dreams and mystical abilities. She and Isis are also seen as two aspects of the same deity, which can be looked upon as dual aspects of the human nature. Nephthys was also credited with being the mother of the god Anubis; the guardian of the dead and one who is employed for protection while travelling in the astral world. This was a union with Osiris which led her to abandon him, only to be nursed by Isis. Anubis was in fact much older in origin himself, from predynastic times. To many he is still the protector and guardian. Isis, who became the supreme deity and eventually took on all the aspects of other female deities, was herself originally a regional goddess of protection.

We have more information of this period, due to artefacts discovered better preserved than those further back in history. The causes can be natural, like constant wear and weathering, to destruction by the people of the time.

Magic, whatever path an individual takes, is one that the individual feels most drawn to and one they can relate to. The later traditions are also ones of a more mystical devotional following,

The worship of Amun Re and the solar Memphite cult of the Middle Kingdom would appeal to those of a more spiritual, intellectual mind. Although throughout Egyptian history there was much ceremony and ritual, it was at its most lavish during this period. Not everyone has the time or the patience for full blown magical ritual and all the regalia that goes with it. This is what we refer to as the solar tradition. Those who follow this tradition work towards a higher spiritual goal with a more intel-lectual approach.

The predynastic primitive path, which we looked at in the beginning of the chapter, works on the raw natural forces of nature and the deities they represent. The constellations play a big role in this magical path. This is the path of the magician and occultist. One such occultist was the great Aleister Crowley who had a natural ability with magic and was not afraid to experiment to develop an understanding and wisdom that placed him in contact with forces beyond this world. With his wife Rose, while at the Great pyramid of Gizza, he made contact with Aiwass who instructed him to write the *Book of the Law* and informed him of the coming Age of Horus, which is already upon us. It is difficult to gather physical evidence of pre dynastic civilization due to the vast amount of time that has elapsed, but what we do have gives us enough to go on.

Students who work within any of the Egyptian traditions will be familiar with zep tepi, the first origins of life. Depending on which cosmogonies we work with, it will take us back to the very beginning, where all life began. This is a basic grounding and starting point for any would-be student.

The Temple of Khem is a school of the Egyptian magical tradition that gives the student a good grounding in Egyptian magic and guides them to their chosen path. It is always said of any tradition it is the deity that chooses the student and not the other way around. The Temple of Khem has been acknowledged for teaching the genuine history of Egypt, which is based on factual information from The Archaeological Society and similar organisations. The course, which requires a lot of study as well as practical work, helps the student towards their path. All paths within this tradition are if the student wishes to learn. It is all down to them if they are willing to put the work in.

Egyptian magic, as well as this great empire's wonders, will be with us for years and years to come. Because of its vastness and power it will never leave the human subconscious.

Martha Gray is a practitioner of traditional witchcraft and a senior tutor of the Coven of the Scales, and trained in the Egyptian magical tradition of the Temple of Khem. She is the author of *Grimalkyn: The Witch's Cat* and lives in Derbyshire, UK.

Male Witchcraft

Dancing Rabbit

Introduction

When I accepted the task of writing about witchcraft from a male perspective I didn't realize how difficult it would be. Who am I to be the spokesperson for all male Pagans and give the definitive definition of what it is to be a male witch? There are several books out already on the subject of Paganism and witchcraft for men. Those authors have already done an excellent job of covering the subject. I wouldn't want to just rehash what they have said. So, instead of writing a chapter prescribing what male witchcraft could or should be, I have written what I consider to be a few of the distinguishing features of my own practice. Whether this is something specific to male witches or perhaps even typical of witches in general, you, gentle reader, must decide for yourself.

Since I have just mentioned Paganism and witchcraft, let me digress a bit right here at the beginning so there is less confusion later on. I identify myself as a Pagan or more precisely a Neopagan. My religion, my spiritual path, is based loosely on the pre-Christian polytheistic/pantheistic religions of western Europe. I use the word "witchcraft" to focus on the use of magick and casting of spells. While I do works of magick as part of my spiritual path, it is by no means the sum total of that path. Further, I know people who would identify their religion as Catholicism but they also practice a folk magick whose Spanish name translates as witchcraft. Then there is a whole cluster of problems with the words "witch" and "witchcraft". If I were to say to some people, "I am a witch," they would think I had lost my mind since for them the word means something that doesn't really exist. There are witches in the movies, TV shows and fairy tales but anyone who actually believes they are a witch is more than just a little bit out of touch with reality. For others, the word means someone who does evil or harmful magick or someone who is in league with Satan. I am not that either. The concept of a supernatural being of total evil has no place in my view of the world. So for those reasons, I rarely refer to myself as a witch but since you, dear reader, are smarter than the average bear and will not misunderstand what I mean, I will tell you right now that, yes, I am a witch.

Immanent Deity

A number of years ago I was dropping my wife, Feather, off at a women's spirituality camp out and as I was unloading things and setting up her tent one of the women approached me and struck up a conversation about The Goddess. When I told her that I too worshiped The Goddess she was shocked and said that she'd never heard of a man who worshiped The Goddess and didn't know that men could. I smiled and assured her that we could and I did. I think that her ignorance was due to the fact that she had been introduced to The Goddess through feminist spirituality and may not have been aware of the larger Pagan community.

I met The Goddess at a Unitarian summer camp where I also met my wife, my domestic goddess. I was a recovering Christian fundamentalist newly become an agnostic Humanist who had discovered that not only was I welcomed by the Unitarians but so were Pagans. This bothered me at the time because I thought I had found a rational refuge from supernatural religion in Unitarian Universalism and here was the ultimate in superstition: Pagans who practiced witchcraft and believed in magick. Ever open minded, I signed up for two workshops on Paganism and was surprised that this was anything but irrational supernaturalism. Paganism and Pagan witchcraft don't have to do with the supernatural but rather are means of touching immanent deity in the natural world through ritual.

The Mother Goddess, whom I experienced in those workshops, was not a female version of the Christian Father God. She was immanent in all creation. It was about experiencing Her rather than believing in Her. I could experience her in nature and the cycle of the seasons. I could experience Her in other people and in the cycle of birth, life and death. I could experience Her in my own life, in the deeply feminine qualities that I possess. I could experience Her in ritual and in ordinary life. There was no sharp boundary between the sacred and the secular. As in the words of the song, "Everything is holy now." She could be thought of as symbolic, archetypical or as an actual spiritual being or both at the same time. What mattered was whether and to what extent the conceptualization worked and not whether it was true in some absolute sense. I think that the idea of immanent deity along with the orthopraxy that it involves is one of the distinguishing features of modern Paganism. It certainly is for me.

Early on my image of The Goddess, the feminine divine, was drawn from the writings of the neo-Wiccan authors whose books I read. I chose to call on Her as Brigid because Brigid is a Celtic goddess and triple in nature. While I still draw a great deal of my practice from Wicca, I began to add more from historical Paganism and my own personal experience. Ultimately, I dedicated myself to Cerridwen whose nature as both the wise and kindly grandmother, and the strong, sometimes severe crone more fit my own nature and practice.

A few years into Paganism, I felt the need to connect also with the divine masculine. I think it is pretty common for Pagan men especially those of us who came out of Christianity to first identify with the Goddesses and then only later with the Gods. I was drawn to the continental Celtic god who is commonly called Cernunnos, the horned or rather antlered god of the hunt. He too is immanent. He is as near to me as the taste of salt upon my tongue or the bones of my every meal. He is the holy masculinity that is both wild and free yet kind, brave and self-sacrificing.

My book, *The Way of the Horned God,* is not so much the definitive volume on this most masculine of Gods but an invitation to the reader to get to know Him personally. Since writing the book, my thoughts about the Horned God and my relationship to Him have continued to evolve. This past Beltain I realized that the words of the old chant are true. He is "the horned hunter and hunted". He is not simply to be invoked and expected to show up. He must be hunted, pursued, tracked down with no small amount of physical effort. He also actively hunts His children. I spent some time that weekend running and walking in the woods in pursuit of Him and in the end He found me.

Ritual is where I most often meet my Gods. It is a way to shift from the usual logical, linear consciousness into a more holistic, more childlike consciousness. I believe that ritual may be the other most significant contribution that modern Paganism has to make to the world. Yes, I do works of magick but the craft is not the main focus of my path. My main focus is my relationship with the gods, with nature, with other people and with myself. I practice magick and know it can change things but I find that most often magick changes people and people change things.

Honor the Earth

While I do works of magick and honor the gods in ritual, a major part of my path as a male witch involves just getting out in nature and honoring the Earth in practical ways. I live a few miles from the center of the fourth largest city in the U.S. but I spend time regularly in our small but deeply shaded by a huge live oak tree back yard. I keep a small organic herb garden and raise a few vegetables. Feather and I compost what can be composted and recycle much of what can't. We buy our electricity from a company that generates it from 100% solar and wind power. I do a lot of walking and bicycling around town when I can to cut down on our carbon footprint. We both look for opportunities to do random acts of kindness and senseless acts of beauty. Not out of guilt or obligation but out of the joy of occasionally being able to be the change we want to see.

Living in the city and having a demanding day job, I don't get to go camping and hiking in the woods as often as I did when I lived in a small practically rural town. This means that I make sure to appreciate the big tree in the backyard, the small patch of garden and the waning crescent moon in the east as I go to work early in the morning. It also means that the time I spend a couple times a year camping out at the festivals I attend is all the sweeter. I also enjoy getting out in the woods with the Pagan men's circle that I'm a part of and doing guy stuff, like shooting fire arms at targets, felling dead trees with a chain saw, moving heavy things from where they are to where they need to be, improving the festival grounds and sitting around the campfire talking, telling stories, drinking and singing with other Pagan men. In their eyes I see the Pagan gods and their words I hear the gods speaking.

As modern Pagan witches, we need not try to live exactly like our ancestors did hundreds or even thousands of years ago. It is neither possible nor desirable. We must live here and now where we find ourselves but we can still have that grounding connection to nature that they had. It will look slightly different. We will have to plan it and be more intentional about it but we can have it. We must have it.

Ethics

My witchcraft is more than just myth and magick, nature and good deed doing, it is deeply rooted in my personal ethics. Early on, I accepted the Wiccan Rede as holy writ. Since then I have begun to view it as more of a starting place, a piece of sage advice rather than an absolute commandment. I still consider whether my actions and words will harm those around me. I still try to help rather than hurt when possible. I think one of the main reasons that the Rede was made a part of Wicca was that many people might try to do hurtful things with magick that they would never have done otherwise. I might get caught and imprisoned if I shot someone I was angry with but if I put a curse on them and something bad happens to them, who is to know I did it? The Rede was there to remind Pagan witches that magickal actions had consequences just like mundane actions. I see karma or the Rule of Three as more the natural consequences of our actions both magickal and mundane than a spiritual accounting system that metes out rewards and punishments. Quite often the consequences are a change in one's own character for the better or the worse.

The truth is that while magick is more subtle than physical means, the kind of energy that would have be raised to curse someone would definitely do damage to the witch who was doing the cursing if not the person being cursed. That being said, just as there are rare circumstances where physical harm must be inflicted to prevent a greater harm from occurring, I now believe that there are also times when spells designed to harm or control may be justified. My contact with local brujos and root doctors has taught me that sometimes one has to do what must be done. When that is the case, do it quickly and be prepared to accept the consequences.

As a witch and a man, my ethics goes beyond just not hurting people without a really, really good reason. It means that I can enjoy the many harmless pleasurable things in this wonderful life without feeling guilty. So long as it doesn't hurt myself or anyone else I am free do as I will. It means that I can freely decide to help someone without either feeling the compulsion to give till it hurts or feeling the need to make them over as I think they ought to be. I can decide to help or not help without guilt or regret. I can choose when and how I pay it forward. I can have fun and take a rest when I need to. And that is good, for life is too short and too precious to be lived otherwise. I firmly believe that we do not quit playing because we grow old. We grow old because we quit playing.

Conclusion

In conclusion, I'm not sure that my spiritual path of Paganism and witchcraft is typical of the paths of other men and I'm not sure if it is drastically different from that of female witches. You be the judge. I believe that it does have a certain masculine feel or vibe to it and whether you are male or female that you will find that some of it resonates with your own spirit. Take what you will and what works for you. Leave the rest for other. Bright blessings and blessed be.

Dancing Rabbit is a practicing Pagan. He was co-founder of the Elder Grove and currently is co-facilitator of Rhythm of Life Chalice Circle. He is the author of *The Way of the Horned God*.

Witchcraft Tomorrow

David Salisbury

At the time of this writing it's been sixty years since Gerald Gardner's revolutionary book *Witchcraft Today* was published. To say that much has changed since the publication of that book would be a massive understatement. Although I do believe that Gardner had a vision for how big Wicca and witchcraft might become in the future, I don't think he could have ever imagined the heights that it has actually reached. Throughout this book you've been given a deep understanding of where witchcraft was when Gardner was practicing and where it finds itself today. Our next step in understanding the nature of this great movement takes us into the realm of speculation and imagination. The realm of the future.

The progression of the witchcraft movement has been strange and unpredictable over the past sixty years, which makes charting its future a difficult task. I think the best way to do it is to ask questions of ourselves and see where the answers take us. Sometimes we'll have answers to those questions and sometimes we won't. And sometimes the questions will simply lead us to even more questions. Witchcraft is often called a "mystery tradition" so I think this approach is appropriate. When we think about the future of a movement as vast and quickly-changing as contemporary witchcraft, how do we even know the right questions to ask?

That part is a little easier – we start with what we consider to be important and fill in the blanks. I've picked out certain areas that I think are important for any movement and are most likely going to be considered important for a large number of practitioners. I'm not looking at this from a sociologist's perspective, but from a practitioner's perspective. Try as they might, I don't think that even the best sociologist is well-suited to speculate on the future of witchcraft as well as witches themselves. Now, let's take a tour through the future!

Population

Currently it is very difficult to calculate an accurate number of witches and Pagans in any country. Currently in 2014 in the United States, the ability to identify yourself or your family as a Pagan or witch is absent from the US census, the system we use to calculate demographics in our country. But other non-government agencies have conducted independent polling that suggests that Wicca in particular is quickly on the rise. Some polls indicate that in some areas it is the fastest growing religion of all, even beating Christianity and Islam!

If the suspected current rate of growth continues at the pace it is going, that will be the most influential change to our collective future. Everything else that I write about in this chapter will be affected because of our populations. Most Wiccans and witches will agree that our ways are not for everyone and many wince at the idea of Wicca becoming a major religion. But regardless, its unprecedented growth is something we need to prepare for, whether you're excited about it or not.

The continued burst of interest in witchcraft will also have an impact on other religions. A church that would normally have the membership of an entire family would not get the membership of that family any longer. Converts to Wicca from other religions will see their numbers decrease as well. I make that assumption not in the hopes that any other religion is harmed in the process, but as a simple observation of how shifts in religious populations tend to ebb and flow.

Finally, it's interesting to note that the growing numbers in the Pagan movement are unique, and not just because of how fast it's all happening. It's unique in that Pagan religions tend to shun proselytization, which means we do not actively seek converts.

Not many religions and spiritual practices today can claim that!

Infrastructure

Today in the United States where I live there are Pagan community centers, libraries, and land projects in Wisconsin, Minnesota, South Carolina, California, New Mexico, New York, Delaware, and Washington DC. That is not even counting the many Thelemic lodges of the OTO across the world. One of the most well-known Pagan land projects in the US, Circle Sanctuary Nature Preserve, was started by Rev. Selena Fox in Wisconsin shortly after Wicca started to take root in the US. Since then, having a place for witches, Wiccans, and others under the Pagan umbrella to gather has become a top priority for many organizations and individuals.

If the growth of infrastructure continues in this way, it is not crazy to imagine that in another twenty years witches will own properties in so many areas in the US and UK that most people will be able to get to one within a very short driving distance. It's even possible to think that towns with larger populations of witches and Pagans will each have their own type of center, temple, or land space, enabling access through walking (which is great because the cost of gas might be too expensive for most people by then!).

Right now, just about everyone under the Pagan umbrella has to come together to create a Pagan infrastructure project, which gets shared with all of our various traditions. As our different populations grow, it's likely that each religious and spiritual tradition will want their own unique space. So instead of seeing the words "Pagan community center" like we see now, we'll see signs like "10 miles until the Wiccan temple" or "turn right for the witches' community covenstead."

With the increase in infrastructure, it will be much easier for the non-Pagan public to gain access to education about our traditions and who we are. This will foster a new age of understanding and contribute to a decrease in discrimination cases and harassment.

Visibility

As our traditions are exposed to a greater number of people and our populations continue to grow, more and more people in the public eye will begin to openly admit to practicing Wicca, witchcraft, or some form of Paganism. Currently, you can count the number of openly-Pagan mainstream celebrities on one – maybe two – hands. When a celebrity speaks of being a witch now, it is usually something that turns into an amusing and quirky part of their already-strange image. Many of them are rock stars or people who already practice what would be perceived as an "alternative lifestyle" so the public doesn't get into too much of an uproar about it. But can you imagine what will happen once more mainstream celebrities admit to practicing the Craft?

People look up to celebrities and idolize them in one way or another. Whether we think this is a good thing or a bad thing, we cannot deny that they influence public thinking in powerful ways. The more mainstream celebrities that practice (and admit to doing so), the more the general public will be inclined to look into the practices. More young people will likely become involved with the Craft in this way. This is not to say that the celebrity witches will proselytize their practices, but their increased openness and visibility will have that result nonetheless.

Leadership

Leadership is a complicated topic in witchcraft today. Some covens and groups are highly structured, like the Gardnerian and Alexandrian traditions with their various degrees and initiations. Others take a more ecumenical approach by having an intentional lack of central authority. Both approaches have their ups and downs and some groups will change their entire structure around every so often as they figure out what works best for the individuals involved.

In terms of the larger presence of Wicca and witchcraft across the world, it's well known that there is no "Wiccan Pope" or official "King of the Witches", but could there be? Leadership and structure is considered a sign of maturity in any movement. It's possible that as the decades progress, we'll see more councils, summits, and leadership positions in varying roles. I have no doubt that this would be a bumpy road, of course. Pagans tend to feel uncomfortable around leadership, being left with a bad taste of it from previous religious experiences.

While I don't think it likely that there will ever be any Wiccan version of the Vatican, I do think that we will see some changes in the value and importance of leadership. Visibility, which we've already discussed, will be part of that. As leaders become more exposed to greater amount of accountability, it will be a little harder for leaders to abuse power. We've all heard horror stories about abusers creating covens for the purposes of exploiting members sexually and otherwise. Taking leadership more seriously could lead to more effective demonstrations of that leadership.

Since most forms of witchcraft and most traditions of Wicca encourage members to achieve individual autonomy and sovereignty, I suspect that the power of the individual will always be considered paramount. But as our movement grows and gains more exposure, the need for leaders and facilitators will grow along with it.

Scholarship

Back when Gerald Gardner was busy spreading the word about Wicca, it was hard to come by books and research material about the occult. Now there are thousands of books and many organizations entirely dedicated to the subject. There are even entire conferences and professional journals dedicated to advancing

Pagan and polytheist studies that are getting wide, mainstream attention. Some major universities are creating degree options in subjects like Pagan Studies, Contemporary Pagans, and Witchcraft History. While I admit that I'm not much of a scholar myself, I can't help but become very excited about the progress that's being made in Pagan and witchcraft-related scholarship. If education is a signpost of a well-advanced society, then our traditions are certainly on the way to making their mark.

While scholarship and education are definitely advancing, there is much to be desired. We still don't know enough about the religious life of ancient civilizations to accurately reclaim most of them. That is certainly the case with witchcraft studies. With witchcraft and magic considered so malignant throughout history, it is difficult to know what the witches of yesteryear practiced and what their intentions were. It is my hope that advancements in archeology and religious history will reveal more about older occult practices in America, Europe, and elsewhere.

What do we stand to gain by advancing scholarship within our movement and traditions? Status could be a powerful advantage here. Any tradition that can pull from historical accounts while also steadily reinventing itself stands to gain much in the way of respectability and longevity. I predict that institutes focused on scholarly research will become well-estab- lished influences. These institutes will stand alongside other scholarship institutes and work together on common research projects. The resulting coalitions will gain witches and Pagans a table at all of the world's great religious scholarship ventures.

Youth and Families

Wicca is now at an age where those initiated in its early years have grandchildren and even great-grandchildren. As the years move on, there are now more and more individuals born into families that practice Wicca, witchcraft, and other forms of

Paganism. This is a natural part of our community's maturity and growth process and one that will grow rapidly as more decades pass. Many witches and Pagans I know who have children choose to not raise their kids in their tradition for different reasons. Many of them reason that they'd like to raise their kids with information about all paths and then let them decide what they'd like to dedicate themselves to when they're older. Others refrain due to fear of persecution. As we've already discussed, persecution is becoming less and less of an issue as acceptance continues to rise.

I predict that family life will change tremendously for witches in future years. For one, I think raising young witches will become more common as the practice gains common exposure. With the increased amount of temples and community centers in every town, families will have more opportunities to build a Wiccan spiritual structure into daily social life.

Raising children with Wiccan values could cause huge changes in the way social structures involving youth operate. Values like equality, kindness, compassion, and personal power could make kids feel more confident in life while also encouraging them to treat others with more respect. And, of course, growing up with an understanding of kindness and mutual respect would have an equally powerful impact on their lives as adults (which affects the entire community as a whole).

Government

The United States, where I live, has a "separation of church and state" policy that seems mostly to only exist on paper. Everywhere we look there are signs of Christianity as the dominant religious force driving the nation. We see it every day when presidents thank God in speeches or when schools sponsor flagpole prayer circles to Christ. This is changing, although very slowly. Every year we see cases where a Wiccan priestess gives an opening prayer at a city hall meeting, or a student who stands up against attempts at forced prayer in school.

Personally, I'd like to see all religion removed from the government altogether. But that is unlikely as people take religion and spirituality too seriously to be able to remove it from every trace of a system as large as the government. As we envision a world where witchcraft is a major and common influence in society, it is only reasonable to suggest that it will have an influence in different governments.

I think the influence of witchcraft in the government will start small and work its way up from there. We will see more small government leaders like city councillors and mayors coming out as Wiccan and Pagan. Such occurrences are usually made out to be scandals, but increased acceptance will change all of that. Candidates for different elected positions will start to realize that saying you're a witch won't necessarily destroy your campaign or put your political career in the bin. After that, we'll start to see legislators like senators and members of parliament coming out as well. The "family values" that most politicians use as a platform could be helped by saying one is Wiccan, rather than be burdened by the fact. From there, anything is possible. Who will be the first witch president or prime minister? Only time can tell.

Tradition Identity

Although I have no hard numbers to draw from here, it seems that the majority of practitioners of contemporary witchcraft practice in a very eclectic style, rather than under the guide of one particular tradition. In Wicca's early days, you were either a Gardnerian witch, or a "traditional witch" (meaning, not practicing any form of British Traditional Wicca). With the explosion of books on the topic, particularly works by Scott Cunningham, people began to feel encouraged to train themselves and practice as solitary practitioners. This is what I feel caused the onset of today's highly eclectic culture in witchcraft.

In looking at our future in this topic, we are looking at whether witchcraft will become more eclectic, or more traditional. I'm not going to argue about which option I feel will bring witchcraft a brighter future. Instead, I can only look at current trends and make guesses at where it will end up. The difficult part of looking at trends I've seen in my own communities is that I have seen people reach in both directions. I've seen people involved in a specific tradition split off of that tradition and become more eclectic. I've also seen eclectic practitioners crave the feeling of structure and mastery that a tradition can give and move towards that.

In evolution studies, it is said that most systems move towards more diversity, not less. We see that in the melting pot of our countries and cultures, mixing together more and more as the years move on. Whether or not that will play into the traditions of the witches of tomorrow is anyone's guess.

Geographic Communities

If you're in the camp that believes we will start to get more tradition-specific, then it will be easy to imagine that the witches of tomorrow will begin to stick to themselves more and form intentional communities out of those relationships. I believe this will happen with all Pagan religions and traditions in the coming years as we're already seeing that happen now in some cases. Individuals who practice Asatru and Heathenry are forming intentional communities by moving into the same neighborhood. They are intentionally raising families near each other so they can support one another in the process. Their children are already growing up and marrying, further solidifying the bonds of their communities. The act of people coming together to form intentional communities is a longstanding part of history. A great example of it is the early 20th-century immigrants to America from Europe, which gave us the many Jewish, Irish, German, and Italian neighborhoods in just about every major city on the east coast.

The result of intentional communities would have the type of long-range effect that we see in other intentional communities today. Coordination in community efforts will be easier since people will live closer together. Communication in those efforts should be smoother since there would be more opportunity for face-to-face interaction. One could argue that the advancement of technology will pull us all further away from face-to-face communication, but I like to think that Wiccans and Pagans will still appreciate speaking to one another in person when given the chance.

Intentional communities will also spring witchcraft and Paganism forward culturally. Wiccan and Pagan neighborhoods will be covered in art that expresses our collective spiritual interests. With the vast amount of talented artists in our communities, I am in awe when I think of how glorious the art, music, and dress will look in these intentional neighborhoods. You can see this somewhat in places like Salem, Massachusetts, where many of the city's inhabitants follow some sort of Pagan path, which is well apparent in the art and culture of the city.

Economy

Just a quick glance at the industry numbers show that retail purchases for items relating to Wicca and witchcraft generate millions of dollars each year. That is not even including ticketed events, psychic and spiritual readings done by witches, and other miscellaneous services that Wiccan and Pagan leaders offer their communities. In a very short amount of time, modern day witchcraft and Paganism have proven to be a strong forces within today's economy.

The growing population within our communities will have a huge effect on the global economy, especially in the UK, US, and Australia, where these influences are already widely felt. More practitioners means more demand for supplies that many of us need or like to have. The candle industry alone will be in its glory! Not to mention the large number of independent Pagan artists who make crafts and tools by hand that relate to daily and occasional spiritual practice.

Our increased influence on the economy ties in to many of the other topics we've already discussed. Politicians tend to listen to a group of people more when they have more campaign money to donate. The same goes for companies and non-profit organizations that have a say in the way things and ideas are marketed and sold.

Professional and Hobby Associations

In our theoretical world of increased awareness of witchcraft and the Pagan movement, I also predict that we will have our own professional associations and hobby club organizations in every area of interest imaginable. There will be Pagan associations for video gamers, hairdressers, actors, lawyers, physicians, gardeners, football players, bus drivers, city planners, and just about anything else you can imagine. Many associations already exist in some areas, but with our increased numbers, we can expect to see these multiply quickly.

The increase in these associations could ensure increased protections from discrimination for employees in these fields as well as a chance for those interested in these subjects to come together socially, increasing community bonds across the Pagan movement. Niche conventions could be held as another chance to bring people together face to face. This facetime will bring about new ideas, blossoming creativity and progress across all areas. This positive cycle will feed on itself and become self-sustaining, like we see in many niche hobby and industry associations now.

Our Bright Future Requires Action

Everything I've discussed here may sound lovely and wonderful, but it will not come about on its own. Although we have a certain amount of natural momentum on our side, none of this will flourish without all of us taking action now to create this future. Witchcraft did not stop as a growing interest when Gerald Gardner passed from this world because the people he left behind took his legacy and built upon it.

You may not be excited about certain topics highlighted in this chapter, or even agree that their occurrence is a good thing at all. That is perfectly fine. What's important is that you use whatever unique talent you have and bring that to our collective table. The world needs the art of the witches to survive and thrive and it's up to us to ensure that happens.

David Salisbury is Wiccan clergy within Coven of the Spiral Moon, a coven based in Washington DC and author of *The Deep Heart of Witchcraft*.

Part II

Journeys on a Crooked Path

Maria Ede-Weaving

When crisis finds us and our life's reference points shatter – when the map is burnt and signposts fall – we are presented with a startling opportunity to create our world anew. I came to witch-craft via this challenging route.

My journey into this life-affirming spirituality began with my first encounter with the Dark Goddess. I was thirteen and my mother was dying of cancer. In my distress and confusion, I sought solace in what was to become a sexually and emotionally abusive relationship with someone older. With my mother's psychological and physically deterioration and subsequent death, combined with the damage inflicted by the abusive relationship I had become embroiled in, my known world began to disintegrate.

Bereavement and loss can dismantle us; we can feel taken apart, our substance gone. The life we once comfortably occupied can feel alien and without meaning. Raised as a Methodist, my first instinct was to turn to my faith. Church elders could say little to make sense of the devastation I was experiencing. Nothing in my teaching to that point had prepared me for the visceral nature of death or the wounds inflicted by another's cruelty. I yearned to find spiritual comfort, a revelation that might set these events above random fate. The meaning I sought would not present itself for years, although I now understand that the seeds of my Pagan journey began in those moments of crisis.

I searched for a decade to fill the space left in my psyche by the absence of faith. Spiritually homeless and passing from one path to another, I found approaches along the way that intrigued me but failed to find a sense of true belonging within any specific belief system.

In my early twenties I met a Wiccan priestess. Our

conversations triggered a shift in that elusive search. That encounter led to my discovery of a book by Caitlin Matthews entitled *The Elements of the Goddess*. Within its pages I discovered the feminine Divine, a concept that drew me powerfully.

It was to take another five years for the figure of the Goddess to become a vital, living force in my imagination. At university the opportunity arose to take a module outside of my degree programme. *The Female Face of Religion* explored ideas and philosophies of the modern Goddess movement, its core belief the concept of Divine immanence. Raised as a Christian, my perception of the Divine was purely transcendental – God sat outside creation. I became aware that my psychological dependence on the notion of transcendence had made me an enemy of my own body, distorting and damaging any sense of belonging in the material world; moreover, it had made dealing with the pain of my mother's death that much harder to heal. I realised with unnerving clarity that since that awful time in my teens, the world, my body, and even life itself, had felt like a dangerous and unpredictable obstacle to the seemingly pain-free attractions of transcendence. I had internally polarised my physical being and my spiritual life in an effort to transcend my suffering, inadvertently blocking out the beauty and wisdom life on earth could offer.

The significance of the Goddess' immanence in the universe was clear: all aspects of life were an expression of her divinity, including suffering, illness and death; the darker elements of life were not divisive polarisations defined by notions of good or evil, but points on a spectrum; each part of a wider, complex, and varied whole, rich with meaning.

I began exploring the fertile space shared by both feminist spirituality and witchcraft. What had started as an intriguing set of ideas now became a spiritual reality. Building a relationship with the Goddess as she manifested herself through the cycles of sun, moon and season, I discovered that the myriad expressions of her being were reflected not only in the natural world, but also in the unfolding narrative of my life. The elegant and richly layered mandala of the Wheel of the Year grounded her in the world, my body and psyche. Not only that, I discovered that she gave life to an expression of male divinity that was immanent too. The sacrificial God of my childhood fleshed out and became not only redemptive but sexually potent, fertile and joyful. He travelled the journey of seed, blossom, fruit and falling leaf shared by all creation; a deity as close to the events of my life as my own living and dying.

I had needed to find a place for the darkness I had encountered and witchcraft offered not only deity that encompassed all life experience, but myths of descent found in the story of Persephone and the seasonal tale of the Goddess and God. These myths articulated the process of finding ourselves stripped of our psychological scaffolding, a condition brought about by the removal of things cherished and vital; they taught about an honest confrontation with death and loss, and at their heart were the gifts of renewal and transformation.

The Mysteries of Samhain and the Dark Goddess were my entrance points onto the Witch's Path; lessons vital for me to learn if I was ever to find peace, integration and acceptance. My early contact with death had instilled in me a fascination with the shadows. However, none of us should ever become prisoners of a season: life cannot thrive in a perpetual autumn or endless spring. The Wheel of the Year taught me to engage with the changing face of nature and the flow of living, reaching deep into the season of any moment to grasp its essence and its gifts. The search for gnosis – for a deep inner knowing – that witchcraft inspires, depends on some intimate interaction with these agents of change. The joy of this beautiful, elegant spirituality is that it encouraged me to strive towards wholeness, integrating the lessons and wisdom of both the sorrow and the joy and, in doing so, discover a more authentic relationship with life and self.

Kevin Groves

A number of early events in my childhood brought me to where I am now. I grew up on the edge of Deal, in Kent, on a rumoured Roman burial site, from the mid 1970s. Early in our arrival on this new housing estate we all noticed the presence of a ghost. In fact, as the years went by, the ghost appeared to be more focused on me, and through this time I didn't feel threatened. It had plenty of chances to do something bad if it was malevolent, but no, I felt it was trying to gain my attention for some reason.

Then around the early 1980s I discovered two books in my primary school library. The first contained classic ancient Egyptian stories and myths, and these exotic and wondrous tales of those animal-headed gods kick-started a life-long drive into all things Egyptian. The second, which has always been somewhat perplexing, was a book on witchcraft, containing all manner of spells that seemed to resonate with me.

The seeds were sown, those books did indeed rock my 10-year-old mind, and I knew, I felt deeply, these were important. With the very odd out-of-body experiences I had on a regular basis, very scary precognition, and of course this ghost, something was happening in my life. Although I had no idea what it meant, I knew it was going to be significant.

As the next few years went on while I explored my experiences, the wonders of Egypt, and many fruitless attempts to interpret what this ghost wanted, there came, on one trip to a local Sunday market, a marvellous thing. I encountered yet another book on Egypt. This one was the catalogue to the tomb of Tutankhamun, full of amazing colour photos, but it was the statue of Selket that utterly held me spellbound. The moment I saw it I believed it was the most beautiful work of art I had ever seen. I still do, but for quite different reasons now, for it took a few events over the next couple of years that tied the ghost and this statue together, and finally bound my past, present and future to it.

There were a set of revelations that allowed this ghost and I to finally communicate and so it was reveal that this ghost is the goddess Selket and she watches over me and it is now time for me to undertake training with her, mostly through developing my imagination, taking me to wonderful vistas of my mindscape and beyond through projection.

Over time our connection has developed and so too my understanding about many things and myself. The path continues to amaze me and although she is my primary spiritual focus, due to her constant presence, my path continues to remain as a solitary one, partly formed because she is so focused on me. Few others have I found scattered around the planet with similar experiences to share. Perhaps the biggest reason for my solitary path was born out of lacking influence or awareness that there were others, that I later became to know as Pagans or witches, out there that I could talk to and seek guidance from.

I was well on my journey before I had such opportunities to converse with fellow practitioners, although I was taught to embrace any opportunities that come my way and never stand still. My path continues to evolve, so who knows where it will take me? I am very grateful that although I wasn't looking for a spiritual path, my goddess found me. I have found someone who I can walk this path with together, perhaps for eternity.

My practice has evolved in the 20 years since the connection with Selket was established, although predominately continues to revolve around meditation, visualisation and projection, a long-running thread of healing has of late risen to significance.

I continue to read, to learn, to talk with others and the methods have changed and will continue to change as I find use for various tools come and go, and I feel it is still important to constantly review them.

Labels are a difficult thing and I do acknowledge both the

path that originates from my love of Egyptian magic and the land that I live on via traditional European witchcraft practices, of which I tend towards celebrating only Beltane and Samhain, with Samhain being significant due to amplification or strengthening of the connection between my goddess and I. As far as my Egyptian path goes, I mark the summer and winter solstices. I don't feel the need to mark any other traditional festivals. As far as I am concerned, all that matters is the connection that I have with my goddess and our continuous conversation, be that talking or through invocation/evocation practices.

It is a continued conversation, without end, and so long as I acknowledge her in everything I do then I walk the correct path.

Romany Rivers

Death has been my greatest teacher, my most constant companion, my guide on the path I now tread. From my earliest years I have had a love-hate relationship with Death, but when asked to review my path into witchcraft I cannot deny that Death has been the influence that most shaped my journey. Death has changed my circumstances, opened doors and gifted me with opportunities. I stand as the woman I am today, the witch I am today, because of that influence and those opportunities.

As a young child, my brother died. His death and my mother's grief changed my living circumstances dramatically. I moved from my mother's care to my father's home, and spent far more time with my wonderful grandfather. Granddad Tom was Romany Gypsy blood, full of big smiles, a kind heart, and knowledge of the land that seemed magical to my small eyes. I loved to run rampant across my grandparents' small holding, collecting eggs and feeding goats with my grandmother. I made mud pies and perfumes from picked flowers and rainwater. I would take lunch to my great-grandfather who spoke in pidgin Romani-English, patted my head, and crossed my palm with silver coins. I learned about the seasons, the plants to eat or avoid, and the sound of foxes on the common land around their home. I learned about the love of animals, the cycle of life and death, about healing, about killing and eating. I learned about respect, strength, tolerance, anger, and standing up for your beliefs. I learned about sowing seeds, both literal and metaphorical, and reaping the harvest when the time came. I learned that life was hard work, honest work, and worth every moment.

One day, not long after her birth in this world, my sister died. My father and stepmother were devastated, and their grief impacted my brother and I in ways I can only now understand as an adult. My brother was young, and processed death the way that toddlers do, but I was at that cusp of childhood where life moved from play to seriousness. Her death tipped me over from childhood to the awkward limbo of adult responsibility far beyond my years. I packed away my toy dolls and looked after my baby brother as best I could whilst my stepmother sat, and cried, and journeyed deep inside her own pain. I watched our family process grief in many different ways. I heard variations of what happened to the dead, and I sought to understand the concepts of heaven and reincarnation. I reached out with my senses and felt the presence of my sister's spirit hovering around our family, and I struggled to explain that she was still with us to family members who did not want to hear it. Time passed. We grew, and our family grew.

My siblings born after her death grew into toddlers, into children, into little members of our family who demanded time and attention. Still I could feel my sister's presence. Still I saw glimpses of her as her spirit altered and matched her age had she lived. I watched my younger siblings talk to her and play with her, and I watched my stepmother's face blanch white when she understood that it was not just I who felt her presence. Our house was haunted, and family friends avoided us. Family discussions happened behind closed doors, and my name was mentioned as the cause of unrest. Lights would turn on and off, the TV had a mind of its own, objects would move, things would disappear and reappear, words appeared on walls, the dogs followed my sister's spirit when she moved. Over time, it became habit to ask my sister to return lost items, or to say her name in exasperation when pranks were played. Despite her lack of physical presence, she remained influential in our home. Her death taught me so much, and her spirit still teaches me. I learned to feel, see and communicate with spirits. I learned to trust my instincts. I sought answers to the mysteries of life and death in orthodox and alternative belief systems. I studied eastern philosophy, divinatory arts, psychology, parapsychology, meditation. My childhood was hard and often scary, but I learned much from the pain and I grew through it all.

My path to adulthood was eclectic on many levels. I left home young and sought to find myself through work, study and travel. I travelled extensively and spent time with spiritual people from all over the world, every encounter feeding my soul and helping me grow. I was spiritual and practical, hardworking and creative. I found friends who brought out the best in me, and many of them are Pagans.

Slowly I was introduced to more specific paths with Paganism, and I reveled in the sense of familiarity that I found. No longer was I struggling to reflect upon belief systems, instead I found belief systems that reflected me. Wicca offered me the clearest reflection, and I immersed myself in any books I could find on the topic. The equality and balance of the feminine and masculine divine sang to my soul, the ritual practices inspired me and the sabbats and esbats connected with my Gypsy under-standing of the cycles and seasons in a deep and profound way.

Despite the connection, despite having some wonderful Wiccan friends and mentors, I resisted the traditional lineaged method of learning until Death spoke to me. My dear friend, a wonderful witch and one who had been encouraging me to dedicate myself and study Wicca, suffered the horrific pain of losing her son during pregnancy. I knew this as it happened, deep inside my own body. The world moved around me, every-thing pushing outwards and collapsing in again like a visual sonic boom. I felt the loss occurring inside my belly, and I doubled over in pain. I knew it wasn't my pain, and my subcon-scious mind told my conscious mind everything it didn't want to hear.

As awful as it was, it was one of the most deeply spiritual experiences I have ever had and one of the few times I have been so strongly connected to another human being. I went to my friend as she grieved, and it was no surprise to her that I knew, that I felt and that I understood. We cried together. Then she lifted a book from her bed, hit me on the head and said, "I told you. You are a witch. Deal with it."

To this day, my spiritual sister is still helping me deal with it.

David Oliver Kling

My encounter with Wicca started in a manner not unlike many people. I read a couple of books that were available in the late 1980s while in my late teenage years serving in the US Navy. I read a couple of books and became an "expert," or so I thought. Before I joined the Navy I found myself at a drive-in movie theater with some friends getting ready to watch a movie, the name of which name escapes me. My friends and I were talking and before I knew it I was handed a Tarot deck with the explanation, "Check this out." This was a transforming moment for me. I had never been indoctrinated into any particular faith, but I had a genuine respect for all faiths. Having this Tarot deck in my hand unlocked an understanding within me that, "I am a spiritual being," and I reference this point in my life when I realized my spiritual potential.

What followed was a lonely life in the Navy as a self-proclaimed Wiccan and Pagan. I did read up whatever was available to me; however, what I had was knowledge. I lacked a strong faith. I had become adept at dabbling. I wanted to go deeper, but without a teacher it is problematic to go deeper. I lacked guidance and direction. So what did I do?

I developed an affection for Roman Catholicism and a deep appreciation of Marian devotion. The experienced I had with Catholicism didn't seem that much different from the Goddess-centered spirituality of Wicca that I had been reading about. I had been attracted to a very conservative strand of Catholicism known as the Traditionalist Movement. Everything was done in Latin as it had been done before the changes within the church that occurred in the 1960s. It seemed very mystical to me and that was attractive. When I got out of the Navy in 1992 I joined a monastery, Christ the King Monastery, which was located in Alabama and took the monastic name of Frater Wolfgang. I remained at the monastery during a probationary period known as postulancy and became a novice monk; however, I left before I was in vows. Something just didn't seem right. I had always been open to ideas and appreciated oneness rather than division and Traditionalist Catholicism was very "Us vs. Them" – a concept I could never truly embrace.

After a brief sojourn with Byzantine Rite Catholicism after leaving the monastery I found myself again alone spiritually. What was different now was that I had experienced faith in community. I understood what it meant to be in communion with others and I took this new perspective to a new level. I was drawn back into the Craft through a religious experience in an odd place.

In 1996 I became a Freemason. Within Masonry prayers are ended with, "So Mote it Be," and this means of ending prayer and supplication took me back to when I was a young sailor and learning about Wicca. It was through Masonry that I re-entered the Craft and reconnected with the Paganism that had lain dormant within me.

Finding a coven and other Pagans was difficult. I looked for several years without connecting with many other people, but I was growing in my reverence for the Lord and Lady. My knowledge was now coupled with religious experience and I saw the Divine with many faces. I had found a couple of people who were willing to share religious experiences together and we formed a coven. Trinity Coven was born in 1998. I used my unique religious experiences and combined it with what I had read over the years to form my own tradition. It was a joyous time of exploration for me.

Eventually I would branch out within Paganism and the Western Mystery Traditions. I found myself involved in Druidry and in addition to being High Priest of a coven I found myself leading groves sponsored by various Druid orders. In 2004, at a Druid festival, I was consecrated a bishop in a Gnostic Christian order. This opened up another transformational period for me. I had found an opportunity to reconcile the Catholicism of my youth with the Paganism of my present and have been on a "Christopagan" path since that transformative time. This was a reflective and introspective time for me that ushered in a lot of change.

In 2004, shortly after my father passed away, I decided to go back to school. In 2008 I finished college with degrees in philosophy and religious studies followed by being accepted into a mainstream Christian seminary. While in seminary I served, as consulting minister, a Unitarian Universalist congregation near my school. It was wonderful opportunity to be able to preach on a wealth of different topics some of which were unapologetically Pagan. After seminary I worked for a year at a hospital studying chaplaincy and spiritual care of others. I discovered the importance of spiritual care and how important it is to the Pagan and Wiccan community.

Every chaplain needs to be endorsed by a church or denomination. I'm endorsed by Sacred Well Congregation International, a Wiccan church, as a minister and cleric priest and I find my path has come full circle. The Craft has claimed me once again. I have always been attracted to acquiring knowledge, but I have come to appreciate and value practical wisdom that comes from listening to the silent whispers of the Goddess through the subtle nuances of nature and finding peace. I have come to appreciate the value of listening to others, of seeing the Divine in the eyes of the people I encounter, and listening to my heart as well as my mind. The Craft has reclaimed me. So Mote it Be.

Katherine Cotoia

I was brought up Roman Catholic and attended Catholic school. Being brought up in the Catholic religion makes you fearful of many things, divination and witchcraft being at the heart. It is tough when you realize that so much of what was taught to you is simply not true. When I purchased my first set of Tarot cards I pictured God shaking his head sadly saying, "Another one lost".

As I got older I always read anything I could get my hands on regarding witchcraft in history, unfortunately these stories were about persecution and death, not something altogether welcoming. The internet was a blessing for Pagans everywhere. As I read more about the old ways I realized that this was what I had been waiting for spiritually. I bought myself a notebook and began writing down everything that I could find on the Craft. I filled that one quickly and began purchasing five subject notebooks so I could separate the different things I was interested in. I still have all those notebooks and I love going back through them and reading my thoughts and interests at the time.

Many years ago I met a practicing witch through my job. I was thrilled! I had never met anyone who shared this interest in the Craft in person before. This was a woman I worked with and had much respect and admiration for. This wonderful woman encouraged me to take the final steps to dedicating myself. I had been reading and studying for so many years, what was I waiting for? I put her off for a while saying that I wasn't ready, the weather wasn't right, whatever excuse I could come up with. Finally she told me, "Just do it and stop worrying". It was time for me to choose my patron Goddess and start planning my dedication ritual. I decided that my Goddess was going to be Cerridwen; I loved her story and felt she was the Goddess for me. I understood a mother's deep love for her child and wanting to do something to help that child in life. I picked the night of a full moon; it was radiant and bright in the night sky.

When all was said and done I felt nothing, nothing at all. I wanted to hang my head and cry. I couldn't believe it, I had expected so much more. Did I say something wrong? Was I truly not ready or was I way off track somehow? As I sat there staring at the sky I noticed this star that was so much brighter than the rest, it seemed to grow and shrink in brightness as I watched it. Suddenly this star seemed to be dropping from the sky heading right towards me! At first I was frightened, then simply mesmerized. It would seem to drop out of the sky towards me and as soon as I became frightened it would then retreat; this went on for a few minutes until it dawned on me, I called on the wrong Goddess! I need a Goddess of the stars and sky!

I quickly cleaned up my tools and began my search for this mysterious star Goddess. I began my search online reading about any deity that had any connection to the stars and came up empty handed. These were not my Goddesses. I had to keep looking. Luckily I am an avid reader and have many books on the Craft. Over the next few days I began going through all of them and finally found her in *Celtic Myth and Magic* by one of my favorite authors, Edain McCoy. As soon as I saw her name I knew it, this was my Goddess. The beautiful Arianrhod.

However, why her? Why a woman who denied her own child and then went and made his life more difficult?

I am the exact opposite; a nurturing, motherly woman who can't seem to do enough for her children. I immersed myself in Arianrhod and read everything I could get my hands on regarding her and anyone whom she was known to have contact with. I put myself in her shoes. I tried to understand why she did the things she did. I encourage everyone to do this with their personal deity. Walk their path in your mind, only then will you truly be able to connect with them. On another full moon evening I dedicated myself to the old ways and named Arianrhod as my personal Goddess.

I do not know if I can fully explain the feelings that I experienced that evening. It was truly a feeling of peace and enlightenment, this was the feeling I had searched and longed for over the years spiritually. This is the path I was meant to follow; there was no doubt in my mind. By the time I finished I had tears streaming down my face. I had finally come home. Over the years I have called on other deities. However, Arianrhod is and always will be my patron Goddess. She called out to me in my time of need and led me to her. My deepest love and respect will always be hers.

Being Pagan has delivered many gifts to my life. If I had not opened myself up to this path I do not believe I would be who I am today: an herbalist, aromatherapist, organic gardener, spiritual counselor, mother, and wife. I grow my own herbs and botanicals to use in my creations. I love being able to help people find their spiritual path. I truly love who I am. I am confident in myself and my beliefs. I am always striving to learn more as there is always something to learn in life. While this path may not be for everyone, know that there is a path for everyone. Find your path, seek your own enlightenment in this world.

Pamela Norrie

Childhood is a very magical time, everything is full of wonder and surprise. We see the world with fresh eyes, and everything is an adventure, a new discovery, a new delight. But over time we lose some of that sense of wonder due to growing up and social conditioning. We take the world for granted and instead we try to fit in by doing as the majority do. But for some of us, we still manage to seek out the magic even when others consider us old enough to know better.

I didn't follow trends and I didn't care about the latest pop bands. I was busy dreaming up magical worlds and looking for faeries at the bottom of the garden. I believed in magic and always thought the witch in fairy tales was given a bad rap. To me there was magic in every leaf and flower, in the air, all around. That seemed more real to me than anything else. So using the wonders of my imagination, my seven-year-old self would concoct potions using everyday items, and write my own spells for fun. Some were a bit more unrealistic than others. (I never managed to get the hang of the flying spell – I must have put in too much shampoo.)

As I reached my teenage years I found information about psychics and fortune telling, ghosts and reincarnation through magazines and newspapers, and the feeling of magic had never left me. I read all I could find. I knew there was a lot more to the world than what I had been taught, and I continued to hunt down information.

Everything changed at age 14, which seems to be a common age for many people finding their spiritual path. I came across a magazine written for teenage girls and inside it had a few articles about "spooky" things. There was a review of a spell book – a well known purple velvet bound book. To think there were actual spell books in publication, that someone out there also believed in magic and found a way to practice it and get it to work! Of course I had to get that book as soon as possible. Using my pocket money I rushed to my local bookshop and wandered into a section I'd never noticed before – Mind, Body, Spirit.

To my surprise there were dozens of books on magic, witchcraft and ritual. This was exactly what I had been looking for. I rushed home with my purchase – which wasn't the purple velvet book, but another by a different author which contained more content. I didn't just want to know how to cast spells. Nope, I was going to learn as much as I could and do it properly.

After spending many evenings holed up in my room reading, and then buying more books and devouring those as well, I started to define myself as a witch and it felt right. Some of my friends were a bit unsure, and my family thought it was a fad. But as years passed and my interest never waned they began to accept it. Solitary practice has its ups and downs. The good part of it is you pace your own study, and you set your own parameters. The down side is there are no teachers to answer your questions, authors contradict each other leaving you confused, and learning comes from trial and error. It can be a very lonely path.

I continued as a solitary working occasionally with a friend or two for several years. The idea of joining a coven seemed impossible, and I did yearn for more training. However, I had heard some frightening stories of what can happen when people join covens – High Priestesses on ego trips, abuse, manipulation etc. I began to think perhaps it was best I remain solitary.

But after 11 years of solitary study I felt I had reached a plateau, and each new book I picked up said the exact same thing as the ones before. I didn't know how to progress from there. My life was in a state of turmoil too – family problems and being under stress and working full time. I longed for a way to sort out my life and advance in the Craft. I longed for a teacher, someone with more experience. It seemed my call was answered when I met another witch in a local New Age shop (and there had been several things happen to lead us to that meeting, *no coincidences*).

We sat down for a coffee and I found out she was a member of a local coven. When hearing of my fears about covens, she quickly reassured me that was not the case, and through her I was put in touch with her High Priestess. I got to meet the others in the coven, and was bowled over by how much they cared about each other, how sincere they were. I realised then how much I wanted to be a part of that, and later I was offered training and entry into the coven.

The training wasn't always easy, but I learned to face my fears, and confront the darker aspects of my psyche. I was aware of my own ego's whisperings and sought to keep it in check. The training filled in the gaps of my knowledge from solitary work, and I was ecstatic with how much I had accomplished in my year and a day versus 11 years of self-study.

Working in a coven isn't suited to everyone, and I don't place it above what I learned as a solitary. Experiencing both has enriched my life and my practice, it has shaped me into who I am today. So there are no coincidences. I truly believe I was brought to the Craft because I dared to look further, and when I sent out a call, the cosmos answered back.

Halo Quin

I've always been fey, in the sense of not quite "normal". A little different, sensitive, prone to daydreaming and disappearing into other worlds. I spent most of my childhood looking for fairies and, when asked what I wanted to be when I grew up my primary response was, in fact, "A faerie". Childhood dreams can come true...

Growing up I was taught to respect life. Plants have feelings and should be treated with compassion. Litter was a serious offence near my mother, and trees were the divine incarnate. On the flipside I had the Church of England. I wrote prayers to God, I polished brass with granny and sang in the choir with grampy. For my ninth Christmas I begged for a copy of the Bible and was disappointed in the children's version I was given. I wanted the magic words. I wanted the real power, the sacred text. I learned two things from these religious parts of my upbringing: 1. Life is sacred and 2. Words have power. As a result I always strive for honesty and compassion. I recognise the life in the rest of nature and the importance of a tongue that does not lie.

Aged 10 I discovered ghosts. A story from a friend, scared by her experiences, sent me to the most holy place I knew: the library. In the place where words live I looked for books on ghosts but the book entitled *Witches* was the one that captured my attention and opened a whole new world...

From that moment on I devoured every book I could get my hands on and through books and my spirit guides I learnt about the magic in the world. Despite the fact that it was ghosts that opened the doorway for me, it was faeries that led me deeper in. Each one of us resonates with certain energies and for me, as I said, it has always been them. It was searching for faeries online that ultimately lead me to Reclaiming... via one of that tradition's central magical roots: Feri. I am not an initiate, but through Feri work with Gabriel Carillo and T. Thorn Coyle I trained to strengthen the soul, to clean and clear and forge the spirit and mind into a whole being that can step out into the world and live in tune with the Divine Will carried in our hearts. This root lead me to Reclaiming events, Witchcamps, where I learned to co-create magical space and community, and where I found the power of stories explicitly stated. These two modes of making magic – clarifying and strengthening one's core and co-creating magic in the world – helped me to grow strong.

The year 2009 rolls around and I find myself in Spain, sharing the work that sang in my soul, leading a workshop on finding Faery within your heart. The story of that camp was Thomas the Rhymer, the tale of the man who enters Faeryland and leaves with the tongue that cannot lie, and it changed my life again. That weekend I went from dreaming about the fae to writing about them, from working with them to sharing gateways to fae magic. Here was when all the threads of my life came together and my own magical path coalesced into something with a clear shape… the FeyHearted Path. You could say that this was the point that I learnt to leave Faeryland and to take my truth into the world.

My previous explorations had led me to an understanding of what it means to be fey and who the fae are. The fae are the wild spirits, the untamed magic, the consciousness of nature, the spirits of the plants and the magic of the otherworld that lies closest to our own land. Because we are a part of nature, we hold that wild magic in our hearts too. When we understand which parts of ourselves are masks and which parts are our true heart-song expressed, we can choose to follow the magic in our souls. We can hear the song of the universe and we can act accordingly… following the music of Faery and finding adventure, healing and great treasure. Those of us that are fey, knowing the difference, can choose when to wear those costumes or to discard them, we hear the music of Faery beating in our hearts and we follow it further than others ever imagine. At each step in my path I've felt guided to uncover those distinctions, to explore myself and return to the authentic core while keeping only those masks which are useful and burning those that do not reflect my authentic self. This is the work that came together in the FeyHearted Path, under the guidance of Thomas the Rhymer, The Queen of Elphame and the magic of the land of Wales.

All life is sacred and words have power. The stories we listen to, the tales we tell, shape our lives, shape the world. We strengthen ourselves and then create community and change in the world. The music of Faery beats in our hearts and we fey ones listen, we follow. I followed. The fae are creatures of surprise and sometimes I look back over a life of chance encounters, accidental discoveries, random choices and I see the hand of their Queen leading me to where I am now. I am an Enchantress. I wove together the threads gifted to me and spun myself a new tale... always following the music of Faery.

If you are wandering into witchcraft I invite you to look back over your life... what is the common thread? Whose is the hand that guides you? What thread, when you pull it, is the one that always takes you forward? If you uncover the song of your heart and the magic that calls to you then you will always be able to follow it home... and if you hear the music of Faery in your heart, I'd love for you to join me on the FeyHearted Path.

Cher Wright

My soul has always been Pagan. However, I was born into a Pentecostal family who attended a church that controlled the thoughts and feelings of their parishioners. My parents' marriage was not one founded on love. My father, an addict, showed up at church one day with a friend and the pastor went to my mother, a young, overweight girl of 19, and told her God spoke to him. God wanted her to marry this man and placed a responsibility on her head to "save" him. Three months later they were married. Another three months and I was conceived.

I believe I have always had a strong connection with spirit, even if I was not always listening. Before I was born, spirit saved my life. My mother couldn't sleep one night and was anxious. She felt she needed to get out of the house right away. After much effort, she finally convinced my father to take her for a drive. The two of them went for ice cream and talked about how "the baby" might change their lives. It was a very pleasant night and when she felt calm, they returned home but found a shocking scene playing out. Fire trucks, flashing lights, smoke; our home was burnt to the ground. The landlady had fire bombed their rental home for the insurance money. A fire fighter informed my parents that had they been home, they would have perished. God had saved them, and me. Spirit allowed me to be born.

November 18, 1971. I came into this world loud and full of stubbornness. My first outing was to church. My mother was sure to do what was expected and raise me to be a good Christian girl and devoted me to the congregation at the Gospel Tabernacle. I was measured from that moment on to the standard set by the strict views of our church.

In our belief system, to question anything was a sin. Sin – such a tiny word that held the weight of a thousand solar systems. I bore that word on my soul like my own personal cross. I was sinful. I didn't fit. I questioned everything. I couldn't pray like the rest of them. Instead, I talked to dead loved ones. It just felt more natural. I believed in reincarnation – though I didn't have that word in my vocabulary yet. Even at the young age of five, I knew I had been here before and would be here again. These ideas did not sit well with the members of the church. Something had to be done to save my soul. They informed me that I was a backslider.

It was time to use fear. That was the retaliation for questioning the ideas and philosophy of the church. "Accept" it or be condemned to Hell. This technique worked on me outwardly. I became a perfect example of an obedient Pentecostal woman. A loving, devout follower of my teaching. Inside, I was terrified because I knew I wasn't "right". I was different. So, I lived a life of self-correction and was desperate to be like everyone else. I grew up, got married and had children. Always pretending that it all made sense. But inside, I was feeling completely wrong and afraid.

One day I wandered into the New Age aisle of a book store. I felt the eyes of God and all the angels burning my skin as I chose a book and walked up to make my purchase. Although the words written on the pages felt as if they came straight from my soul, my programming got the better of me. Evil, sin, hell, disappointment – those words rattled in my ears until I threw the book out and once again denied my calling.

I went back to the life I knew. My journey derailed, but my fear was alleviated. My life went on. However, my connection to spirit would not let this derailment last for long. Spirit has a way of guiding you to the right path. I acquired a thirst for the study of ancient civilizations and cultures. That can't be sinful; you can't go to hell for studying history, right? Oh my, what a world was opened up to me. Through this study, the ancient spirits of gods and goddesses were finally able to speak to me. Slowly they healed my wounds, took away my fears and opened up my heart and mind. Slowly, they drew positive Pagan role models and teachers into my life.

A beautiful journey lay out in front of me. Bit by bit, I left behind the world I knew and traded it for this one. A life filled with magic, wonder and equality. Spirit sent me a mentor, Doris, who told me to stop doubting myself. She helped me to believe that I was absolutely perfect at this moment. "Relax, just let things be," she once said to me. With this advice I was able to learn many life lessons, the most important of which is that I learned to accept myself. I am now happy with my spirituality, though I realize it is an infinite journey. I love the goddess in me and because of this, it's easier to love and accept others as they are. My path has been rocky and filled with perils, but I would not change one part. It has made me what I am, a strong, compassionate Pagan woman. I don't know what is ahead of me on my path, but I embrace the journey.

Salexa Stevens

I was introduced to the occult by a few books a neighbor had given me mixed in with a bunch of Harlequin Romances. I had read them with both trepidation and excitement. I was afraid that just reading the books would strike me blind and curse me for all eternity as my good and loving hellfire and brimstone pastor would have surely said if he knew. I was excited because what I was reading made so much sense to me. They struck a chord within me that sang to my heart. As much as those books showed me a path, they still left something missing. The internet had yet to be made available to the general public, occult stores had yet to come into formation, and surely none of my friends shared the same interests. Some cringed in horror when I brought the subject up or showed them the books. I was alone in my discovery.

This proved to be a blessing. I had no choice but to learn on my own. I was my only teacher. When I called on the Goddess I pictured in my mind the great ladies from fiction and mythology. I conjured up my own images of what they would look like. I have always felt the magick in the time between night and dawn, and between dusk and night.

It was many years later I was to learn that the Celtics call this time Imbus. But also I had felt the magick in the time before a storm, or induced by dancing with abandon. My magick came from my instincts, and as my instincts grew stronger so did my magick. I admit it was with great joy years later when my beliefs and feelings were validated by the writing of others.

Nowadays you can go on the internet or perhaps just down the street to buy your tools, and there is certainly nothing wrong with this. I have seen some absolutely incredible wands offered for sale. I've even bought one for a friend. Yet in my heart of hearts none can surpass the one I made over 30 years ago, it sings to me because I have used it for so long and because in making it I put a part of myself in it.

So many times I hear young Wiccans ask for more learning. They delve deeply and relentlessly into books, the internet, and chat groups, searching for the answers they seek. I have many a time poured over books of herbs, looked on the net for a specific spell or chant. These tools have proven invaluable. But just as valuable and far more powerful have been the truths I have found on my own. The truths that have always been my own, just waiting for me to see them. So while you are working on Wicca 101 or 102, listen to your heart. Believe your own truths, recognize and listen to the truths that have been yours all along, waiting for you to discover them hidden in the depths of your soul.

Craigen Smith

There are two things I wish to cover, the first being how my journey began into my craft, and the second, just what exactly is my craft. Let me start by saying I'm and Ovate of the Order of Bards, Ovates and Druids and I believe that we are the witches of the Druidic cast. Ours is the realm of the deep green forest, where the old trees still talk and pass on their wisdom, of the ancestors and the other realms, of divination, herb lore and healing.

I was sat one day, in my grove, a lovely little spot on a brook, dominated by an Alder, who is defiantly boss, guardian, and protector. I entered my inner grove and was sat on a log, by the fire, my guide was sat with me. He told me I was to set off on an adventure, and not to worry about where it would take me, but just to trust in the journey.

He then pointed to a gap in the trees, that had a path leading from it, one that I'm sure I had never noticed before, but such is the way. I traveled along until I came to a place that felt right, so I slowed and explored my surroundings. I became aware of an old crone sat off to one side. She beckoned me over. I had never seen her before or at least I did not recognise her, she was defiantly not a side of Isis I had ever encountered before, still I approached her. She welcomed me and introduced herself. She was Ceridwen the wise woman, goddess of the witches. She told me that she had a journey for me, if I was happy to take it, with my assent she summoned my staff, and then we were transported to the tree he came from. Ceridwen and the tree spirit blessed and energised my staff. She told me I was to learn the craft of the wise, that I would know the way when it came and that my staff would protect me as I learnt, and with that she sent me off! That was it, the beginning of my travels into the world of witchcraft!

So what is my craft? Well for me it's a process of getting closer to, living with and exploring nature. I do this in four main ways that I shall outline here. The first is by following the Wheel of the Year with my grove mates. I'm lucky to be a member of a fantastic grove. We meet eight times a year to mark the equinoxes and the solstices but also the Celtic fire festivals of Imbolc, Beltain, Lughdnasah and Samhuinn. We meet in a grassy field surrounded by Rhododendron, and Oak, Holly and Maple.

You can really see the year march on, especially as it is somewhere I only go for ritual. Each year I have eight snapshots of the weather, how the trees are doing, the seasons. You really begin to notice the rhythm of life, but as it's a place I only go for ritual I do not take for granted what I'm seeing and experiencing, in the way that we often do as we walk down the street. The festivals not only help me to stay connecting to the movements of the year, but also give me a chance to develop and grow as an individual. Each year I plant new seeds for a better me in the spring and then see how I've developed come harvest. Then, at Samhuinn, I cast off a few bad habits or traits and prepare myself ready for the next set of seeds to be planted. It's a very therapeutic cycle and one that, over the years, I hope has shaped me into a better human being.

The second way that I go about my craft is to make regular offerings in my own personal grove. I do this at least on every full moon, but really as often as I can. I would cast a circle and call in the quarters, then spend some time in meditation or chanting, or working on my OBOD course work maybe. It always amazes me how much these spaces seem to change as you use them for magical purposes. Their energy changes, they become more alive, more peaceful. I would then make offerings to my gods, my ancestors and the spirits of the grove.

My offerings usually take the form of incense, beer, honey, milk and home-baked bread. This is just my way of saying thank you and showing I care.

Every now and then I might write a prayer flag out and tie it to a tree. These are always transcribed into Ogam. Sometimes they contain prayers, or ask for blessings for people or endeavours that I may be undertaking. I like the way they stay as a semi-permanent reminder of what I've asked for help with. Each time I go down to my grove I automatically review how I'm getting on with each. The third part of my craft is talking to trees. There is so much we can learn from them if we only open ourselves up. At the beginning of my Ovate journey I purchased a set of staves made from each of the trees that they represent. It's a lovely set. I sat under an ancient Yew tree with my set, meditating on my journey to come and the tree suggested that I pull a stave each month and set off to find that tree.

Finding them is a huge part of the journey. I'm lucky in that I live in a big city, but one that has a lot of open land set aside as country parks. On my monthly rambles I've been fortunate enough to find all 20 trees. I take with me a little offering for the tree spirits and then just open myself up to them. I sit with them, and introduce myself. I ask them if it's okay if I talk to them for a while, if they are agreeable, and they are not always. I journey into my inner world and go to meet the tree. I ask it questions about its personality, how it feels in its environment, what it thinks it represents. I ask if I can take something back to my altar. Once our conversation is at an end I'll dig out my Caitlin Matthews and Paul Rhys Mountfort book and see what they have to say on the subject. It's interesting to see how the tree sees itself and how we as humans see them. By going through this process I find that I always have a place I can go in the real world, but also a place I can go in my inner would, should I wish to consult with the tree again.

The final part of my craft is to learn plant and herb lore. Sometimes plants are suggested to me, and other times I have a specific need and seek out the right plants. My reference materials are usually either Culpepper or Cunningham. If, however, I'm not working on anything specific, I'll take Kris Hughes' advice and just go to get really close to nature, look at the plants around me and see what they have to say to me. Once I've done a little homework, I'll use the herb, if it's safe to do so. I'll make teas with it, use it in a bath, and burn it as incense. Through doing these things I learn about what the plant means to me and how I can most effectively work with it. It's surprising how over time this knowledge accumulates, and how the more I do the more my confidence builds to move on to other things. And so there you have it, my path to my Ovate craft and how I practice it.

MOON
BOOKS

Moon Books invites you to begin or deepen your encounter with
Paganism, in all its rich, creative, flourishing forms.